Confessions of a Crackpot

Based on Humor/Life Style Newspaper Columns
of MaryLee Marilee

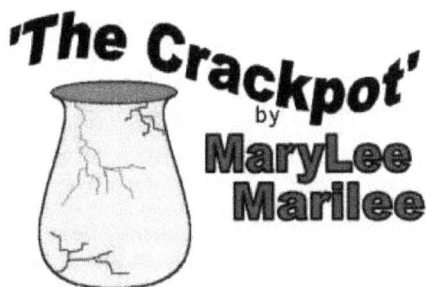

'The Crackpot'
by
MaryLee
Marilee

Paper Bridges
Books

Published by Paper Bridges
March 2014

Disclaimer:

This is a work taken from the Newspaper Columns: *Confessions of a Crackpot, Rolling Along, and The Crackpot,* by MaryLee Marilee, published by Graphic Publications in three to five weekly newspapers from 1994 - 2006. All names, characters, places and incidents used by the author are attributeable to her, and to her alone. Any references to actual people, living, dead (or otherwise incarnate), or to events or locales is entirely coincidental.

If you think you recognize someone within these pages, all I can say (as my old, writing professor used to say) is that "it's all grist for the mill!"

ISBN: 978-0-9831765-9-6   Print Book
ISBN: 978-0-9831765-8-9   E-book

ALSO BY THE AUTHOR:

We Laughed... We Cried... We Ate Dog Biscuits

Based on Humor/Life Style Newspaper Columns
of MaryLee Marilee

The Hearthstones Series
(Historical Fiction)
(MaryLee Marilee with Sheryl Drake Lawrence)

Book I
Keep the Home Fires Burning

Book II
Let the Sparks Fly!

Book III
Glowing Embers

(Available at Amazon.com and BarnesandNoble.com)

CONTENTS:

Soap Box

Travel and Adventures

DEDICATION

For my children and grandchildren—the lights of my life!

I ask their forgiveness for any undue stress as a result of reporting life as it happens.

Hey, that's the breaks when you have a writer in the family!

Introduction

My Cracked Pot

Did you ever have the opportunity to throw a pot? I don't mean winging one across the room, I'm talking about using a potter's wheel to shape a lump of clay.

Watching a skilled potter at work has always fascinated me. So when I had the opportunity to experiment with a potter's wheel several years ago, I had a ball. Maybe the little kid inside, who still loves to get her fingers muddy, made me take an interest in throwing pots in the first place, but something much deeper made me stick with that pottery course long after I'd acquired the necessary art credits, when I went back to college as a "non-traditional student" (better known as the old lady in the class).

Becoming a master potter requires a lifetime of devotion to the craft. By way of comparison, you could say that I'm still in kindergarten dabbling at the "play-dough" level. Don't get me wrong, I've managed to create some nice, functional pots; a few of them even turned out quite beautiful (depending upon the eyes of beholder, of course).

One pot in particular—which I had intended to make into a dog dish—ended up taking its place as my favorite casserole. Hey, you never know what you're liable to get when you start shaping the clay; it's a surprise every time.

The whole process of creating a pot involves much more than simply manipulating wet clay on a wheel. After you form the initial creation, that pot must dry to the "leather" stage, when you can then trim the base and add handles or other clay decorations.

But only after drying completely, does the pot undergo its first firing in the kiln. Sometimes during this heating process, if a pot has not thoroughly dried, it can explode from water trapped inside. Any impurities or bubbles in the clay might make a pot crack, as well.

The particular pot upon which I base this column had none of those problems. It survived its first firing in fine condition, and, after adding glaze, it emerged from the second firing transformed.

It's always a kick to open the kiln after a second firing (the one that sets the glaze). Everything looks so different from what it did going in.

I kept my finished pot on top of the refrigerator to collect "things." You know, one of those catch-all kind of places for keys and rubber bands and twist-ties and fortune cookie messages. My pot sat up there for weeks, doing its job.

Then one day when I was in the adjacent family room, I heard a loud *"PING"* sound, which had come from the kitchen. I didn't have a clue as to what could have made that noise.

I searched the kitchen, looking for a fallen picture or broken glass, some sign of catastrophe, when my eyes fell upon that pot.

There it sat with a long, gaping crack down its side.

Keep in mind that several months had passed since that last firing process. But (according to my professor), an inner tension left in the clay had finally wreaked its havoc and forced that little pot to crack.

My own life has undergone a similar process.

I learned the hard way, what "keeping everything inside" can do to a person. Sooner or later the pressure takes its toll.

I, too, had cracked.

Going back to college helped me begin to piece my life back together at a time when I felt totally shattered and alone. But slowly, I began to learn healthier ways to diffuse the inner tension—whether it be digging in the garden, swimming half-a-mile, hollering at the top of my lungs from the branches of a tree (where no one else can hear, mind you)—*or by writing*.

So I keep that cracked pot as a constant reminder. And whenever I'm tempted to revert to the old, familiar habit of biting my tongue and keeping my emotions trapped inside, I look at my pot and remember the price I must pay to do that.

Internalizing the tension costs dearly.

But as E.B. White once put it: *"Remember, genius is more often found in a cracked pot, than in a whole one."* Although I fall far short of genius status, I *have* gained a unique perspective from the lessons taught by my little, cracked pot.

Through the eyes of this particular *Crackpot*, I humbly come to share my outlook on life through the medium of this column. And I come to share a message with you, as well:

No matter how badly shattered your pot—no matter what your struggles or your circumstances—you can be whole, once again.

Oh, it does take time and effort to glue the fragments back together again. But remember this: the cracks that remain are where the light shines through!

Think of this column as a "cheerleader for the human spirit"—a light shining through the cracks of this resurrected pot of mine, that helps to keep folks moving forward, instead of wandering alone in the dark.

Heaven knows, even the best of us need a little encouragement to "keep on keepin' on."

So, week after week, month after month, and year after year, in my own hair-brained way, I've tried to help folks find a smile, while coping with the craziest foul-balls life has a way of zinging at us.

All the calls, letters and e-mails I've received over the years reaffirm that people in a wide range of ages and backgrounds have related to the boiled-down bites of life I serve up each week.

I've always tried to catch my readers with a good hook, develop a simple concept, proffer a kernel of wisdom to munch, then wrap it all up with a droll twist that can leave folks with a smile—if not an outright chuckle—while addressing all manner of subjects that expose the foibles of humanity.

Heaven forbid the use of moralistic schmaltz! But a slightly "cracked" approach I have done my best to employ without fail.

You never know what this Crackpot is apt to deal out, for you *do* need to understand, I haven't been playing with a full deck for some time!

"Thank you" to all the devoted readers who took time to respond to my columns over the 15 years they appeared in *The Holmes County Bargain Hunter* and its sister papers. I appreciate your faithfulness in reading them all that time. Because of your requests, I offer this collection.

Hey, that's not a bad track record, for something you use to wrap the garbage!

Happy Reading!

CONFESSIONS

Celebrate 'National Ding-a-Ling Day'

Ding-a-lings untie! I mean, unite! It's a day of our very own! (And I'm not talking bell-ringers, here, either, even though Christmas is closing in.)

Now most people would rather swallow a dose of smelly cod-liver oil than admit to ding-a-ling status, but it's a certifiable fact (and any number of people have agreed I'm definitely certifyable) that ding-a-lings possess some of the most creative minds around.

They can come up with near genius methods for reprogramming Uncle Cid's new computer, or reengineering the proverbial mouse trap, but ask them where they put the car keys, or whom they talked to just five minutes ago on the phone, and chances are, they won't remember either.

A ding-a-ling can tell you exactly what Aunt Ethel wore to the New Year's Eve blow-out in 1967, and probably even recount her list of resolutions for '68, but if you expect that same ding-a-ling to remember the babysitter's phone number or yesterday's lunch menu I have to tell you, you're in for a disappointment.

As self-appointed spokes-person for ding-a-lings, I'll tell you why: we don't clutter our minds with facts and figures we can look up elsewhere. We remember those seemingly unimportant impressions and characteristics that no printed reference-volume could possibly hold.

We save room in there for the gears to grind, instead.

And speaking from a writer's perspective, all those feelings and impressions will most likely find their way into a story or column—eventually.

As my old English professor used to say, "It's all grist for the mill." (He definitely qualified as certifiable, too.)

Now you're probably wondering where I'm going with this line of thought.

I'll tell you.

Next time you ask someone what you think is a relatively simple question: e.g., "Where did you put the checkbook?" and they can't remember, don't get upset right away. First, think it through as a ding-a-ling would.

She carried the checkbook outside to pay the Schwan man, and on the way back inside, she tripped over the dog dish, spilling Roscoe's food all over the porch.

Naturally, the first thing she'd think to do, was refill the dish for that poor, deprived canine, so it stands to reason the checkbook has to be in the dog food bag.

Simple!

I know, you're shaking your head, thinking, "what kind of nut would spout all this ding-a-ling silliness?"

Don't ever underestimate the power of silliness. When you feel hemmed in and can see no apparent way out of a problem, try brainstorming for the silliest most outlandish solutions you can come up with.

It might come as quite a surprise, when an idea you thought silly offers the kernel of wisdom that holds the very solution you need.

That's what creativity is really all about. When we give the mind room to work—and the freedom to be silly or crazy or foolish or wild—solutions often present themselves. But first we must loose the bonds of preconceived limitation.

Now I have an important differentiation to make before we go any farther: there's a world of difference between a ding-a-ling and a dingbat.

Though a ding-a-ling may not *appear* to possess any cognitive ability to speak of, a dingbat possesses absolutely no common sense whatsoever.

A ding-a-ling CAN brainstorm her way through any number of sticky conundrums and come up with creative solutions, but the most basic grasp of reality completely escapes a dingbat.

Case in point:

Since I live next door to and share part of a driveway with a llama farm, we do get quite a few "llamalookers" stopping in.

> *It might come as quite a surprise, when an idea you thought silly offers the kernel of wisdom that holds the very solution you need.*

As fate would have it on this particular day when my neighbors happened to be away at a llama show, an older woman pulling a horse trailer drove her vehicle into the driveway and stopped at the neighbor's closed gate.

Now let me affirm that I lead the biggest cheering section when it comes to encouraging the "graying woman" in her pursuit of offbeat fulfillment. That a 60-something woman had the gumption to pull a trailer at all deserves some approbation.

However, any activity involving a vehicle presupposes that the person involved should have at *least* a mediocre understanding of its operation, right? (My first mistake of assumption).

Well, in trying to be a good neighbor, I found out that this particular woman had come about a male llama of breeding age. Hence, I surmised, the need for a trailer. (My second mistake).

Upon discovering my neighbors not at home, she insisted that I introduce her to every male llama on the place. After the better part of an hour, she finally understood the need to leave and come back another day for more reliable information (hey, I do know these llamas by name, but when it comes to reciting sires and dams, I'm clueless).

But now this woman had a problem: in order leave, she had to back up that trailer. And rather than attempt it, she decided to make a wide swing through my rain-soaked yard, rather than back up on a solid, gravel driveway. (You do see what's coming here.)

Naturally, she got stuck. And rather than feather the gas pedal to *ease* her way out of a sticky situation, she gunned the thing and got herself *really* stuck—not to mention managing to jackknife her trailer between a new maple tree and the corner of our house, to boot.

3

After watching as long as I could stand it, I went to the window of her Suburban and said, "Out, woman. If anyone's going to tear up my lawn, *I'll* be the one to do it."

She answered, "All right. But be sure you don't set the emergency brake, because the whole brake system will lock up if you do." (Wonderful!)

Before I could even hope to extricate the trailer, we had to unhitch it and back her Suburban around onto the other side of that tree. But (you guessed it) she didn't know how to go about unhitching a trailer.

O.K. I got the trailer unhitched, the vehicle realigned, reattached the trailer, then proceeded to haul sand for traction in the slippery mud. (Did I mention her tires were practically bald?)

I eased the vehicle forward until I hit slick grass, then I'd haul more sand for additional traction, continuing this procedure as I inched my way up the semi-steep grade in my yard. After about 20 minutes of this, she finally came to the window and said, "Do you think it would help if we unloaded the horses?"

"You mean to tell me you've had *horses* in that trailer this whole time?"

I need mention here that I'd heard not one whinny or kick or snort from any horse, so I had *assumed* the enclosed trailer to be empty in anticipation of hauling home a llama. (Another BIG mistake of assumption on my part!)

I won't even go into the fun we had with aforementioned horses upon removing them from the trailer.

Finally, after considerable time and effort, I did get that trailer unstuck. When, at last, I hit solid gravel in the driveway, I can tell you I did *not* stop until I had that thing pulled all the way out onto the road.

I put the vehicle in park and hit the hazard lights—they didn't work, either!

Needless to say, by the time this whole scenario had played itself out, I was not a happy camper.

The moral to this little story? Only a dingbat would pull a trailer without knowing how to back the thing up (not to mention knowing how to hitch and unhitch it), and with a questionable vehicle to boot.

A ding-a-ling, on the other hand, when seeing no apparent way out of a sticky situation will brainstorm for a solution until she finds it.

(Next time I unload the horses FIRST!).

Naturally, this whole experience—emotional triggers, lasting impressions and all—has made wonderful grist for this writer's mill!

Happy Ding-a-ling Day!

Morning Grrrrrr!

"I feel mad as a cornered she-bear and twice as ugly! So EVERYBODY stay out of my way!"

Do you ever wonder why some mornings dawn with grizzly feelings bristling underneath your extra-sensitive skin?

Normally I'm one of those sickeningly-sweet, bounce-all-over-the-place, morning kind of people whom the grumpies of this world can barely tolerate until they've had at least three cups of coffee to make the day bearable.

On this particular morning, however, I awoke ready to pounce on the first warm body who had the gall to utter any kind of civil greeting. Luckily, the only one in close proximity first thing happened to be Roxie, my dingbat dog.

She managed to deflect the worst of my morning madness before I had occasion to see another living soul.

No matter what kind of emotions emanate from their masters, a person's dog just sits there and takes it, or slinks off out of boot-kicking range to wait out the passing storm.

Nothing seems to faze Roxie—my half Dalmatian, half Chocolate Lab canine of boundless energy. Her muscle-bound tail wags the rest of her 70-lb.-plus body, which gives you an idea of the exuberant welcome I get on any occasion, whether I have thunder booming in my wake or not.

"I love ya, I love ya, I love ya, yeah, yeah, yeah!" (Wag, wag, wag, wag.)

Even when *I* growl at *her*, she still looks up with those googley brown eyes full of love, waiting for a pat on the head.

Maybe her unswerving attitude has something to do with that hard head of hers meeting up with the pavement, when a passing semi sent her rolling a few years back. Knocked all the attitude right out of her and left a dithering dingbat in her place.

Don't get me wrong, I love her to death, even if she does happen to be the most screwball dog I've ever owned.

Thankfully, Roxie manages to smooth off the sharp edges of my moodiness before I have occasion to interact with any person in my life who really matters to me.

Try as I might, though, I can't explain the unusual anger that had me in its grips when I awoke today. I do remember some mighty wacky and upsetting dreams rolling around in my cranium just before my eyes took in the first rays of morning sunshine.

But how can something as intangible and ethereal as a dream cause a person to jump up fighting mad, like a snarly-toothed mama bear giving her all to protect her cubs?

I ask you, how can a simple dream affect one so?

Maybe it has something to do with the stirring of raw emotion we so-called adults manage to keep under wraps during normal, waking hours.

Under the refuge of sleep our true selves can finally emerge, as dreams trigger what's lurking inside, ready to boil over when the guard over our emotions has no opportunity to keep things in check.

Watch a small child sometime. Raw passions play out to their full capacity—from outright joy and sheer ecstasy to foot-stomping fury and heart-wrenching grief.

A child holds nothing back. So why do we adults?

A child lets the emotion roll over and through and out, getting to the other side of it in quick order, then goes back to play as if nothing happened at all.

> *Why have we adults learned to mask what's going on inside of us, in the name of civilized behavior?*

Why have we adults learned to mask what's going on inside of us, in the name of civilized behavior? Does it really serve to make us more happy and healthy in the whole scheme of things?

7

What would happen if, like children, we allowed emotion to play itself out, rather than trapping it inside to trigger headaches, ulcers and all manner of physical ailments that add to *dis*-ease?

While you chew on this conundrum, I'm going downstairs to tackle my dirt-hole of a basement, all covered with ash after a long winter of burning a wood stove. Nothing beats the catharsis of tying into heavy cleaning in order to work off a boat-load of anger.

Hey, it beats kicking the dog! Besides, Roxie would just sit there and take it while trying to figure out how she could swipe my shoe.

So much fabric, so little time!

"She who dies with the most fabric, wins"—that epitaph should appear on every fabricholic's gravestone.

As a charter-member fabricholic myself, I can verify that once the ol' creative bug has bit, you're definitely a goner.

I blame it on my genes, of course—on my maternal grandmother, to be more precise. She, too, loved creating things, and for that familial trait I'm truly thankful.

The creative spirit does, however, possess its downside. You have to find a place to store all the *stuff* necessary to feed such an innovative habit.

If sewing is your creative habit of choice, then the "stuff" of seamstresses everywhere boils down to FABRIC! (Not to mention—needles, thread, zippers, patterns, trims and sewing gadgets of every shape and size.)

Naturally, feeding such a habit means visiting fabric stores. And without reticence I can easily direct you to every fabric store within a 120-mile radius of my home.

However, I think I need to "broaden my horizons" when it comes to the quest of tracking down that perfect piece of fabric. To that end, I've enlarged my search area, and I've come up with a list of 567 fabric stores within the state of Ohio.

(Fellow fabricholics can go online and find that list at http://fabdir.com/ohio.html. If that doesn't give us enough to choose from, we can always broaden the search for fabric stores all over the country!)

Dare I share with you one of my wildest fantasies? I hesitate even to set it in print.

O.K., O.K, you convinced me—I'll tell.

I've always entertained the notion of being set loose in a fabric store with nothing but a bottomless checkbook at my disposal. (I wouldn't mind someone setting me loose in a book store the same way, but I'll have to save that for another column.)

Hey, a girl can dream, can't she?

Besides, after that bug bites and the creative condition reaches a fever pitch, you HAVE to have enough raw material from which to create a masterpiece, right?

Of course right!

My best friend, partner-in-crime, Thelma, has elected yarn as her creative "stuff" of choice. Since she has just come into the possession of a superwammedon, double-bed, computerized, knitting machine, naturally she HAS to build an inventory of raw material from which to make her one-of-a-kind, knitted creations.

But finding handy specialty-yarn shops presents a much greater quest than finding fabric stores. So that, of course, brings us to the online auction site at eBay®, where all colors and varieties of cone yarn abound (along with everything else imaginable under the sun!).

Thelma's bidding habit has become so intense, her husband has threatened to buy stock in UPS just to try and recoup some of her investment. Every time she arrives home from work, another shipment of boxes awaits, stacked at front (or back or side) door.

Naturally, her biggest challenge involves trying to hide all that yarn before her husband comes home!

At least I don't have to worry about pacifying an agitated husband. But I do have to figure out where to store all this fabric.

Hey, you don't happen to have a 22-inch, chartreuse zipper in your "stash" that would go with this hard-to-match swatch I have right here, do you?

How fast were you going, Ma'am?

"I need to see your license, registration and proof of insurance, Ma'am."

"They're right here, officer. But it might take me a minute to find them, buried in my purse." *(Drats, he got me.)*

"Do you know how fast you were going?"

"How fast was I going?"

"Forty-six, then 44, then 42 as you came in over the bridge. Were you in a hurry?"

"No, I was just singing."

"Singing?"

"It's such a beautiful morning, and that beat was so catchy, I couldn't help singing. Here's my license. I found it."

"Is all the information on this current, MaryLee Marilee? That can't really be your name, can it?"

"It can, and it is." (I can see he's not convinced.)

"Weren't you watching your speedometer when you came into town?"

"Well, my speedometer's the problem, you see. I never know if it registers faster or slower than I'm really going. They put smaller snow tires on the back of this little buggy, and they told me it would affect the way my speed registers. But I can never remember if they meant it's supposed to be faster or slower than the speedometer actually shows. I'm dyslexic, so things like this really give me fits."

"Your speedometer's not my problem, Ma'am. Going over the speed limit is."

"At least I was slowing down, isn't that something?"

"Your proof of insurance, please?"

"I know I have it right here somewhere. Let me look in the glove box." (I shuffle around underneath the hair rollers, extra napkins, and telephone charger.) "Here it is, officer."

"Wait here until I check all this out, Ma'am."

What do you do when you're waiting for a police officer to write you a ticket? I decided to clean out my purse. At least it's something constructive. By the time I had everything removed, sorted, and neatly replaced in that receptacle, the officer returned to my window.

"MaryLee Marilee. You were right. It IS your name."

"Would I lie to a police officer?"

"Lots of people do. All right. I'm giving you a warning for your speed this time. Keep it down, from now on."

"Thanks, officer. I appreciate that."

"I *am* giving you a seat belt citation, however. That won't put points on your license, at least. Don't you wear your seat belt?"

"Sometimes I do. Sometimes I don't. Today I don't."

"You need to wear it at all times."

"I know, I know. But tell me, I could never understand why a guy wearing no shirt, no helmet, and NO SEATBELT can ride a motorcycle without any problems from the law, and I, sitting inside a steel-reinforced vehicle equipped with airbags, no less, can get a ticket for not wearing a seatbelt. Why is that?"

> *Why DO we say thank you when an officer hands us a ticket?*

"It's the law, Ma'am. I just enforce it. Here's your citation. You can choose to appear in court on the 15th, or sign the waver and send in payment to this address any time before that."

"All right. Thank you." (Why DO we say thank you when an officer hands us a ticket?)

"Keep the speed down."

"Yes, sir."

"And wear your seat belt."

"All right." (I hook it up as we speak.)

"And if you feel the need to sing, at least keep an eye on your speedometer."

"Check."

"Have a good day."

Have a good day? Well, they're all good, aren't they—even if you do get a traffic ticket!

(Fifty-dollar fine plus court costs. There goes a tank of gas! But at least I've done my part to fill the city coffers, and the ticketing officer can count one more victim toward his monthly quota!)

Improvise

Did you ever play "Improvise?" You won't find it in the game section beside Trivial Pursuit® or Monopoly®. It's the kind of game that you make up as you go along.

I'll give you an example: as newlyweds living in a tiny, furnished apartment near Great Lakes Naval Base, we had little in the way of worldly goods when we set up housekeeping.

Since my sailor husband would be shipped out in one month's time, back in those Vietnam war days, we took the bare minimum of necessities—only what we could jam into our 1964 Buick LeSabre—for our short stay in the Chicago area.

I was young and naïve, trying to impress a new husband with cooking ability I did not yet possess. So the first day, after I drove him to the base at 5 a.m. on traffic-clogged city streets that I did *not* know (a trial by fire for a dirt-road country girl), I decided to surprise him with a home-baked cake when he got home.

Fine. I tackled the project with enthusiasm, but I ran up against several problems right off the bat: I had no baking powder, no eggs, and no cake flour, but I did have a mixing bowl and a brand new cookbook, so I hunted through the recipes for one that made use of the ingredients I *did* have on hand.

Did you know that in a pinch, you can substitute apple sauce for an egg? It doesn't work great, but you can "make do." And if you sift regular flour enough times, you can make it light enough for a cake—of course, sifting flour without a sifter presents quite a challenge.

The only thing remotely close to a sifter at my disposal was a window screen—which, naturally, I washed thoroughly before trying out. You should have seen the flour cloud I created in that kitchen!

After I finally got the batter all mixed up, I hunted around for something to bake it in; I didn't have any cake pans either, but I did have an electric frying pan that came with directions for using it to bake a cake. What the hey! I poured the batter in, slapped on the lid and plugged that thing in.

Half the fun of creation is in learning to improvise with what a person has on hand.

You know it worked! Course, it came out a bit flat, and a little brown on the bottom, but it definitely looked and tasted like a cake. Good. Now for frosting. (I did have ingredients for that.)

But after smearing on that sweet-tasting goo, my poor cake looked a little lifeless, so I decided to decorate it up a bit. But I had no cake-decorating tools.

No problem, I could cut marshmallows into flower petals. Then, if I cut off the corner of a plastic bag, maybe I could squeeze frosting through that to write out a little message. The theory was good, but in practical application, I just got globs of frosting all over the place. I needed something smaller.

So I started looking around the place with a creative eye. I spied an Elmer's Glue bottle with an end that looked just like a cake-decorating tip. Bingo!

By the time I had my creation finished, I had one whale of a mess all over that kitchen. Clean-up time. But guess what? No dish pan. What could I use for a dish pan?

When I opened the refrigerator door, the revelation hit me— use the vegetable-bin drawer. (I also discovered that a shelf from the refrigerator makes a great cooling rack for cookies, too.)

As you can tell, I never let the lack of proper tools stand in the way of creating something. Besides, half the fun of creation is in learning to improvise with what a person has on hand. Over the years, I've become quite a scrounge in that department.

I've learned to make do with electrical tape to repair a leaky radiator hose and fill that empty radiator with lemonade (it was the only thing available at the time, and though it did make a sticky mess, it sure beat burning up the engine); I've cleaned out clogged drains with baking soda and vinegar, plugged holes in drywall with toothpaste, and I could fill up a whole column with uses I've discovered for duct tape.

> *This game of "Improvise" has only one official rule — be creative.*

This game of "Improvise" has only one official rule — be creative.

It sure beats sitting around feeling sorry for yourself about what you *don't* have. Besides, using the right tool at the right time gets boring. Be a little innovative and see what you can use to "make do."

In the process of stretching your imagination, you, too, may come to learn that we really don't *need* much "stuff" to get along in this world.

And if the project you're creating doesn't turn out exactly as you'd planned, so what? Just call that flat cake brownies!

Once, when no one was looking...

Once, when no one was looking, I climbed to the top of Brubaker's silo.

I knew I wasn't supposed to do it, but I did it anyway. That long ladder to the top of the world just called out, and I answered.

Now, this ladder looked like no ordinary, step-type ladder I had ever climbed before. This particular ladder consisted of narrow metal bars, totally enclosed in a little tunnel-like affair that looked like a giant mud-wasp had stuck its home-quarters on the side of that mammoth-sized kraut-jar.

And so, I climbed. And I climbed. And just about the time I got half way up, I looked back down.

Big mistake.

I clung to that ladder with all I had in me, trying to decide whether I should inch my way back down or keep on climbing. Climbing won out. It took me a while, but I managed to make it all the way to the top of that silo.

And when I finally got up there, what a view! I could see the whole world (at least it seemed that way to a 10-year-old kid).

This was much better than sitting in the old maple tree back home. This empty silo shot up a good four or five stories higher than my favorite branch in Cid (that's what I'd named the maple in front of our house).

I loved nothing better than sitting in a crotch of that tree, jammed in real good between two big branches, reading the day away. I'd pretend I was queen of the whole farm, looking down upon my kingdom. But the view from this perch, at the top of Brubaker's silo, outdid anything I had ever seen from the branches of ol' Cid.

Talk about a kingdom. I felt like queen of the world, up there!

I hadn't thought about climbing that silo in years. But today, it seems apropos. My partner and I (better known as 'Thelma' to my

'Louise') have so far tallied up more than 70 rejection letters from New York literary agencies in our attempt to acquire skilled representation in the dog-eat-dog publishing arena for our three-novel historical series.*

We're using our rejection letters to paper a wall.

But the question we face (now that we've climbed half way up this creaky ladder) is do we continue to climb in our bid for the top, or do we get cold feet, call it quits and climb back down to safety.

> *Only when you face down a fear, can you find the freedom you need to keep right on climbing.*

The beauty of this particular literary partnership lies in the fact that not only do we work well together, but when one of us feels a little shaky and uncertain about our common goal, the other one usually has a fire lit under her to keep us both charged and climbing upward. Danger threatens only when both of us happen to reach a doubtful rung at the very same time.

Which brings us to our present situation—clinging to each other in the middle of this hair-raising climb.

But if the lumps I've taken throughout this bumpy trip have taught me nothing else, they've taught me this: only when you face down a fear, can you find the freedom you need to flourish and grow—and the courage you need to keep right on climbing.

Soooooooo, we kiss this next batch of query letters for luck, slap on more stamps, and send them off to the big city with the hope that they'll spark an interest in someone, somewhere, who will finally request our entire manuscript.

Wish us luck! We still have one whale of a climb ahead of us, but it's only dizzying if we forget and look back down!

*Since the initial publication of this column, the aforementioned three novels of the *Hearthstones Series* have seen publication and are available online at Amazon.com or BarnesandNoble.com.

Reaching for a Dream

You got to have a dream,
If you don't have a dream,
How you gonna have a dream come true?

The first time I ever heard Bloody Mary sing those words in Rogers & Hammerstein's musical, *South Pacific*, they hit me right between the eyes: how can you go anywhere or accomplish anything if you don't envision it first?

But there's a catch: the capacity to weave dreams requires an active imagination. And, unfortunately, this hurry-up, keep-the-treadmill-running world of ours tends to squelch creative fancy.

"Stop daydreaming and get to work!" How many times did a teacher scold you with that reprimand? I must admit, I got my share of scoldings for gazing into space in the classroom (which is what my teacher thought I was doing, but inside my head, I was *busy*.)

Without a spark of fancy to kindle those creative fires, how can we ever hope to encourage active imaginations in our children? (Don't *even* get me started on this video-game-benumbed generation!)

Some folks argue that either you're born with imagination, or you're not. I contend that everyone starts out with at least a little spark; some just sparkle brighter than others.

However, it's easy to snuff that spark completely. Precious few reach adulthood with any glimmer of it left at all. (Look into a person's eyes; you can tell when it's dead.)

I believe even the tiniest spark of imagination can burst into flame given the proper coaxing.

Turn off the TV sometime, and see what happens when a child has to use his imagination to entertain himself.

> *I believe even the tiniest spark of imagination can burst into flame, given the proper coaxing.*

Don't acknowledge the complaint every kid will try: *"I'm bored. There's nothing to do."*

Know what I told my kids when they tried that excuse?

"Boredom is the state of an underactive mind. I'm not here to entertain you. Put your mind in gear and entertain yourselves. If you can't do that, I have a whole list of chores right here that'll keep you plenty busy!"

Sounds harsh, but it worked. And now that they're grown, they've all thanked me for pushing them to use their imaginations; for urging them to visualize dreams and reach for them.

"If one advances confidently in the direction of his dreams, and endeavors to live the life which he has imagined, he will meet with a success unexpected in common hours," says Henry David Thoreau in Walden.

You have to dream your castle in the air before you can lower the drawbridge and walk inside.

> *You have to dream your castle in the air before you can lower the drawbridge and walk inside.*

So step off your treadmill, find a restful spot and daydream for a while. (I always preferred to sit in a tree, myself; you get a great perspective up there.)

Let your mind lead wherever it may—you never know what new possibilities might present themselves. Put your imagination to work weaving a new dream—*then reach for it.*

To sleep, perchance to dream

"To sleep, perchance to dream. Ay, there's the rub."
(Shakespeare).

Although the sleep to which Shakespeare alludes in Hamlet's famous soliloquy undeniably smacks of a more permanent nature than the slumber I pursue, the fact remains that it's 2:30 a.m., and here I lie, wide awake—still wishing to lose myself in that elusive state of dreams.

So what's the problem? Why can't I get to sleep?

The bed sags, my pillow has lumps, and these stupid covers keep getting twisted around my feet, and you KNOW how that bothers me!

Besides, I have a crink in my neck, a pain in my shoulder, and now my back hurts like a son-of-a-gun after all this tossing and turning.

"Did you try counting sheep?" says myself to me.

I made it to six-thousand-seven-hundred and thirty three. Needless to say, I've abandoned that exercise in futility.

"How about listening to the night noises of summer? That always has a way of lulling a body to sleep."

I listened to the frogs croak and the crickets chirp as the stars made their nightly appearance. When the croaking and chirping died down, I heard raccoons begin to argue and shuffle along the creek bank.

Shortly after midnight, the hoot owls began to call. Then the far-away yips of a fox came filtering in on the night breeze.

If it weren't so dry, I'd also listen to water gurgling down the run, but our little creek went underground long ago, in this sweltering summer's drought.

O.K., so I've listened to the night noises come and go with the ticking of the clock, and still I lie here, wide-eyed. NOW what do I do?

"You could always get up, you know."

But I don't want to get up. I want to go to sleep.

"Maybe a little snack would make you feel sleepy."

But I don't WANT to get up! *I want to go to sleep!*

"No matter how much you want to sleep, girl, that's just not gonna happen. You may as well go eat that last piece of chocolate cake."

I think I'd rather have a sardine sandwich.

"So, get up and make yourself a sandwich. While you're at it, why not eat that cake, too?"

Now if you live alone, wandering the house in the middle of the night poses no real logistical problem. You can thump and bang around as much as you want to, and you won't bother a soul.

However, when you have a roommate, a house-mate or a bed-mate, wandering to the kitchen in the dead of night can get a little stickier.

At the moment, I happen to live with a very understanding (not to mention mostly deaf and usually sound-sleeping) aunt, so as long as I keep the thumping and banging to a minimum, and she keeps her bedroom door closed, my late-night forays don't often bother her much—unless I step on the squeaky step, and I've learned how to avoid that.

I've also learned that when I open the refrigerator door, it sheds just enough light to manage in the kitchen without illuminating the entire room as if it were broad daylight.

One mustn't be too obvious. After all, it *is* the middle of the night!

Well, I've eaten a sandwich, cleaned up the cake, and had a couple of cookies to boot. Wow, all of a sudden my stomach doesn't feel too great.

"Who in their right mind eats sardines and chocolate cake together," I ask myself.

Perhaps a dish of yogurt would help settle a sour stomach?

"Good grief, it's 4 a.m. May as well put on a pot of coffee and get to work at the ol' keyboard now; you've blown this entire night's sleep for sure, girl."

Do you think maybe tomorrow night I shall find that elusive land of nod?

Coloring between the lines

Has anyone given you a box of crayons and a blank page and told you to "draw a picture" lately?

I'd bet double donut holes it hasn't happened to you since grade school art class.

Remember what it felt like to stare at that empty page, wondering what to draw? I always found it much easier to follow specific instructions: draw a house; draw a tree with a swing in it; draw a picture of what you want to be when you grow up.

Having something concrete in mind gives the assignment a handle—a tangible place to start. Filling up a blank page without directions requires some thought, and that makes the assignment feel like work.

A coloring book, on the other hand, offers a lot more thoughtless fun (especially Christmas coloring books, which are my favorite). Just color between the lines; it requires very little in the way of self-generated creativity.

The pictures in my coloring book never looked as good as Aunt Maryjane's did, though. She used color and shading in a way I'd never seen done before. Amazing, what she could do with a Crayola®!

I had a reminder of the artistic quandary I faced back in grade school, when I was treated to dinner at a unique restaurant not long ago (the Macaroni Grill near I-77 & SR 18 outside Akron—great place, especially if you appreciate superb Italian food and fine opera).

The waiter handed us three crayons as he seated my dinner companion and me at a table covered with a giant piece of blank paper.

"It's all yours. Create!"

"On the table?"

"Of course!"

"But what do I draw?" I asked. "I need to color between the lines."

Coloring between the lines feels safe; the directive to create something out of nothing strikes a chord of anxiety, even in the most relaxed of circumstances.

(Ever hear of writer's block? Same dynamics, different medium, only the pressure to create something is a bit more crucial when you're staring at a blank page with a deadline breathing down your neck.)

I had a difficult time deciding what to draw on my tablecloth easel. But once I started—once I put that first shaky line on the paper—something amazing happened! Swooping lines began to appear all over the page—each piece of the picture kept leading to the next.

Before I knew it, we'd filled the whole table with trees and flowers and sheep and race cars. (I have to admit, I did get a bit carried away and fill up most of his section, too). I was almost disappointed when dinner arrived.

And the fact that we'd already filled our whole paper with "art" didn't keep me from wanting to continue.

> *Powerful things begin to happen when you unleash a creative spirit.*

"See, that table over there? Those people didn't draw a single picture. Let me go fill their page up, too!"

Powerful things begin to happen when you unleash a creative spirit—but only after you've removed self-imposed boundaries.

So now, how 'bout coloring a picture? Get out a box of ol' Crayolas® and see what you can do. And if you get the urge, send me your "creation." I'd love to hang it on my wall right next to all the Snoopy-and-his-typewriter comic strips. (Everyone loves to come in here and read my walls).

I think I'll go home and get out the coloring book and crayons my daughter gave me for Mother's Day (she knows her mother!)

But I'm not gonna stay between the lines, anymore.

Confession of a 'Creative Genius'

I have a confession to make: I'm a compulsive creator. One look in my" creative loft" at all the projects stacked in piles around here might give you a tiny peek into my penchant for creativity.

Without a creative outlet of some kind in my life, I'm absolutely certain I'd wither away and die—not a physical death, mind you, but most assuredly an emotional one.

A pretty sight, that is not. Unfortunately, I've seen far too many people walking around the face of this earth quite deadened, creatively speaking. That's really nothing new, but a sad waste, nonetheless.

So what happens to quench that inborn spark? Where does the imagination go?

Most children start kindergarten intent on learning and eager to create. Yet by the time they reach high school and college, much of their creative enthusiasm has disappeared.

One of my all-time favorite quotes comes straight from the mouth of a college freshman in my intermediate French class, when I returned to school as an "old lady." He sat staring in frustration at our mid-term exam he said, *"Geeze, they send you off to college and expect you to think!"*

> *In order to work, education needs to be an active verb... You have to want to know more.*

In order to work, education needs to be an active verb. A teacher can't just pour knowledge into someone's mind, like pouring milk through a funnel. It takes active involvement.

You have to *want* to know more.

So why do we allow a child's inborn enthusiasm to die?

Robert Fulghum (of *All I Really Need to Know I Learned I Kindergarten* fame) raised this very question in one of his unforgettable essays. When a child starts school, he's anxious to discover more. He says "YES!" when asked if he can draw or sing or dance or try anything new. But by the time that same child becomes a freshman or sophomore in high school, he won't even admit that he can draw or write or sing or create anything, especially if it smacks of individuality.

Heaven forbid that he should be considered *different* from everyone else his age!

Hooey on conformity, I say!

Stop squelching creative genius by pressuring people to conform to the norm. Only when we can fully accept our individuality and acknowledge our unique talents and gifts can we set creativity free.

> *Only when we can fully accept our individuality and acknowledge our unique talents and gifts can we set creativity free.*

And use those talents and gifts we must. For to create is the greatest work "The Great Creator" has given us to do.

Julia Cameron, in *The Artist's Way, A Spiritual Path to Higher Creativity*, gives these pointers to help encourage creative minds to bloom:

* Creativity flourishes in a place of safety and acceptance.
* Creativity grows among friends, withers among enemies.
* All creative ideas are children who deserve our protection.
* All creative success requires creative failure.

Fulfilling our creativity is a sacred trust. Violating someone's creativity destroys that trust. Creative feedback must support the creative child, never shame it.

For example, never ask a child, "What is this picture?" Instead ask, "Would you please tell me about your picture?" Creative feedback must build upon strengths, never on weaknesses.

Success occurs in clusters and is born in generosity. We are all meant to cherish and serve one another.

Albert Einstein said, "(Creative) imagination is more important than knowledge." I agree, but I'd add one proviso: If you don't *exercise* your creative spirit, you'll lose it. And no amount of knowledge can fill the void.

So throw yourself into a creative challenge. And if you can think of nothing more creative than to get out a box of crayons and go to town on a blank page, then do it!

Be sure you fill up that page, too. No staying-between-the-lines coloring-books for this assignment, either. Let your imagination soar so your creativity can flow!

(Drop me a line; let me know what you create and how you feel while you're creating it. Nothing's more fun than the sheer joy of sharing a brain child. Write to **Maryleemarilee@gmail.com**.*)*

Snoopy Writes Again

If you steal from one author, it's plagiarism;
if you steal from many, it's research.
—Wilson Mizner

At the risk of bringing copyright infringement charges down upon my head, I'd like to quote from one of my favorite comic strips—*Peanuts*©. (I have my office plastered with comic strips of Snoopy sitting on his dog house, banging away at his typewriter.)

Lucy says, *"They all do it, why shouldn't you? Just take a famous fairy tale and change it a little."* Snoopy types: *"Snow White and the Seven Beagles."*

(Without the cartoon frames that accompany the words, it loses a little in the translation, but you get the idea.)

I don't know a single writer who hasn't done just what Snoopy did—take an idea or title and change it just enough to make it into something of one's own.

I do it all the time. People tell me I'm creative, but I know the truth—I'm simply good at stealing ideas, giving them my own little twist, and turning them into something that reflects my cockeyed view of the world.

Nothing creative about it. 'Course after tutelage under one of the best (in my opinion) professors-of-writing, Dr. Richard Snyder, and working with relentless Editor Mike, maybe I have come a little farther than I think.

> *People tell me I'm creative, but I know the truth—I'm simply good at stealing ideas, giving them my own little twist...*

I'm indebted to both men for their rigorous instruction. The cutting and tightening process often causes great pain, but it also makes for a much better read. And we are, after all, writing to be read, are we not?

That's what I used to think. But now I know the truth about that, too: I write in order to *see* what I'm thinking. I have to get it organized on the page before I can sort it all out in my head. Sometimes it's a real surprise to see what's in there!

In the process, the writing purges my soul. And once in a while, hidden in all the garbage that comes pouring out, I find a few gems. Not often, mind you—but just often enough to keep me struggling at this heart-wrenching craft.

Dr. Snyder once told me, "Writing will break your heart; it breaks all our hearts eventually."

Yet regardless of the pain, write I must.

So, like Snoopy, I keep hammering away. Whenever I get discouraged at my seeming lack of progress, I just read my walls and take courage from Snoopy's never-say-die attitude:

"Dear Contributor, We are returning your worthless story. It is the dumbest story we have ever read. Please don't send us any more. Please, Please, Please!"

Snoopy says with a smile: *"I love to hear an editor beg."*

A fly's-eye-view of the world

Did you ever stand on your head as a child, or hang upside down over the end of the bed to get a fly's-eye-view of the world? Do you remember what the room looked like from that position, with the door up there on the ceiling and lights down there on the floor?

The upside-down room certainly did *look* different than its right-side-up counterpart. But nothing in it had changed really— only my perspective of it had.

I can remember looking at the world from an inverted position quite often in my younger days—outdoors as well as in. I'd hang upside down from the crossbar of the swing set, or (more often than not) with my knees crooked over the branch of a tree.

As a child I spent so much time climbing trees, my parents surely must have thought I was part monkey.

Now that I'm older, I wonder whether my compulsion to invert things had any basis in the fact that I happen to be dyslexic. The way I see *everything* is upside down and backwards compared to the way most folks see the same thing. (A fact that drives my editor crazy if I'm having a particularly "dyslexic day" when I type. In my head, I see the keyboard reversed!)

When I learned to write, way back in kindergarten and first grade, I can remember teachers working and working with me to "do it the way you see it on the blackboard." I thought I *was* writing it that way, but my paper came out looking reversed to everyone else.

Today I'd probably be labeled "learning disabled," but fifty-some years ago, I was just a "problem child" in the classroom who needed extra help. I suspect that I spent so much time dangling upside down in those days, because I was trying to figure out which way really *was* the correct way to see things.

Eventually I did manage to "do it the way it looked on the blackboard." (The pressure to conform in our world can overwhelm the most stouthearted of souls, let alone one skinny five-year-old.)

Although I do write and read "right-side-up" today, I can still look at an upside down book and read it without difficulty (a skill that comes in quite handy when sitting across the desk from someone who thinks you can't read what he's writing).

If I have trouble making heads or tails out of a difficult situation, sometimes it helps to "invert it" and take a good look from a different perspective.

After I've spent any time at all reading that way, though, I have to stare at a right-side-up book for quite some time before it makes any sense to me again.

I often have to stare at the problems I stumble over before they make any sense to me, too. If I have trouble making heads or tails out of a difficult situation, sometimes it helps to "invert it" and take a good look from a different perspective.

You see, a shift in outlook can make all the difference in the world; defeat really CAN be opportunity turned inside out.

Many moons have passed since I dangled upside down from a tree branch to get a fly's-eye-view of the world, but I did try standing on my head recently, just to remind myself that there's more than one way to look at things.

(For a "middle aged" woman with a bad back, that was quite a feat in itself! O.K., I'll admit it, I did need to balance against the wall to keep from falling over.)

You know, it really does look completely different upside down. Why not try it yourself sometime?

I do still wonder, though, which way really *is* right-side-up?

I still believe in Christmas Magic

Hark! Can you hear it? The carol swells and jungle bells, the falling snow and Ho, ho, hos?

That's Christmas magic in the air.

And before you tune me out, just because I used the "M" word, consider this: the kind of enchantment to which I refer has absolutely nothing to do with sorcery of any kind—unless you also consider the realm of angels taboo.

I ask you, at what other time of year can you use the word, "hark," or talk about the proliferation of celestial spirits and not be whisked away to a padded cell in a straight-jacket?

That's because Christmas magic is at work—Kris Kringle, crafty elves, flying reindeer and all. I'd bet my last button on it.

Now, I realize that many people cast aside the whole Santa Claus tradition. But consider this: what other legend or myth do you know that can bring so many smiles and warm so many hearts as that of a jolly man, bound to give all he has to make children happy?

And who's to say that he DOESN'T exist?

Sure, his work gets done because good-hearted people all over the world pitch in to help out on this one night of wonder. But so does the work of angels. How else do you think we would ever have heard the "good news" unless someone out there was "tuned in" to that celestial music?

The realm of the supernatural shows itself only to those who can suspend belief in so-called reality in order to focus within.

For the abode of angels and elves and fairies lies much closer than you ever realized.

> *The realm of the supernatural shows itself only to those who can suspend belief in so-called reality in order to focus within.*

But very few people have the time (or the inclination) to explore it, because thinking about "things supernatural" makes them nervous, uncomfortable, apprehensive.

"Fear not," said the angel to the shepherds. The very first words out of the box: "Fear not."

"You gotta be kidding!" says they. (Of course they said that. What would YOU say?) Actually seeing and hearing something you can't touch or smell or explain can really give you the willies!

> *Actually seeing and hearing something you can't touch or smell or explain can really give you the willies!*

But the angel said, *"Fear not. For behold, I bring you tidings of great joy, which shall be to all people."* And the angel not only told those shepherds the greatest news this world has ever known, he gave them concrete signs to look for, to verify that claim.

(Wouldn't you want some proof that what you were hearing/seeing/experiencing was real?)

So the next time a child comes to you with a tale that you find difficult to believe, stop yourself for half a beat and consider what people thought when those shepherds told them what they had just heard.

"Sure. Yeah. Right. Of course you heard angels talking. Whaddyya think, I just got off the camel yesterday?"

"Fear not. For behold...."

Children still reside closer to the angel realm than any of us professed "adults." So listen to them. They can help bridge that gap between skepticism and credibility—between cynicism and belief.

Why not let *your* inner child out this Christmas. Go ahead—give yourself permission to "believe" and to "behold." If you can't believe in fairies and elves and Santa Claus, then at least let yourself believe that the angels are watching over us all.

(In case you didn't know it, they're absolutely thrilled when someone makes the jump from viewing so-called *reality* to seeing the supernatural realm.)

Who knows, maybe this year I'll even get a glimpse of those flying reindeer!

Wearing Baubles, Bangles & Beads

"If you get poked with a pin, just holler real loud," I say to my next victim... I mean bride as she gingerly wiggles into the pin-filled dress for her next fitting.

Now if you know anything about sewing (bridal or otherwise) you know that constructing a piece of clothing requires the use of straight pins in order to hold things in place while you fit and sew the garment together.

It's also a given that when you use straight pins, odds are, you're gonna get poked!

There's no way around it.

Since I do a lot of custom bridal sewing (can't help it, I just love the process of creating one-of-a-kind bridal gowns) getting stuck with straight pins does raise a unique problem not necessarily encountered by other kinds of seamstresses: namely the removal of blood stains from white-satin gowns.

(I can see it now when I get audited by the IRS: "I don't think we can allow $220 worth of Band-Aids® as a legitimate business expense." "O.K." I say, "then *YOU* try getting stuck with straight pins and not bleeding all over those white dresses!")

Some people look at what I do and just shake their heads—whether in awe or in disbelief, I haven't quite figured out yet. They ask, "How can you put all that work into a dress that someone will wear for just one day?"

Granted, spending an entire winter sewing beads and sequins onto bridal lace seems inconceivable to some folks (I must have sewn on tens-of-hundreds-of-thousands of those tiny sparkelies during this past winter alone), but I need *something* to keep my hands busy, so why not keep them busy bringing forth a creation of beauty?

"To wear for just one day?"

Yes, to wear for one *special* day—a day that bride will remember for the rest of her life.

On this journey, we get only a few very special moments to see us through the rest of our day-in, day-out existences. And clinging to those few, exceptional moments in the midst of our trials and tribulations can often give us the inspiration we need to persevere.

So yes, I do put a lot of time and energy into making a beautiful bridal gown. I believe that every girl deserves to feel truly ravishing and worthy of love on her wedding day, whether she experiences those feelings at any other time of her life or not.

> *Clinging to those few, exceptional moments in the midst of our trials and tribulations can often give us the inspiration we need to persevere.*

And I can tell you the sad truth—most women never feel so loved or cherished at any other time in their lives.

So, as my next bride bends and twirls and pirouettes in front of the three-way-mirror, looking like Cinderella transformed by her fairy godmother, I smile, take out my pins, and make a minor adjustment in the fit here, take a tiny bit off the hem there, and I revel with her in the awe and wonderment of this journey called marriage upon which she's about to embark.

(Call me the eternal optimist—I still believe it's the greatest journey any two people can take—but the trick is that they have to keep moving *together* in the same direction.)

If you could see these girls as they try on their wedding gowns, watching their dream creations take shape, if you could see the wonder and hope and anticipation in their eyes as they prepare their day of days, you'd understand why I do what I do.

I give the intangible something soft and silky and sparkling to hold on to.

I make dreams come true.

MaryLee Marilee's Dream Creations—has a nice ring to it, don't you think? Hey, I may not come close to resembling a fairy godmother with a magic wand and pixie dust, but give me a seam ripper and few straight pins, and just watch me work a miracle or two!

Is that your phone ringing?

Teedleedleedleeeee! Teedleedleedleeeee!

"Is that you ringing?"

"No, I think it's the guy at the next table."

"The guy's ringing?"

"No, his cell phone's ringing. Are you living in this century, girl?"

"Of course I'm in this century, Thelma. I just try to block out all this cell-phone craziness going on around me. But I have to tell you, it's getting harder and harder all the time. No matter where you go, someone has a cell phone that rings and ends up disturbing everyone around him."

"It's called modern communication, Louise. It's the way the world stays 'in touch.'"

"Well, why can't they stay 'in touch' in the privacy of their own homes?"

"You're missing the whole point, girl. People can talk to each other anywhere, now."

"We already do talk anywhere. We're talking right now in this restaurant."

"I mean they can talk to someone who's not with them, any time they feel like it. You don't have to be tied to a phone wire in the house anymore."

"So, if you're in the middle of a conversation with someone, in a restaurant, say, or in a business meeting, whenever your phone rings, you just leave that person sitting while you talk to someone else? I think that's downright rude."

"No, no, no. It's not like that. Think of it this way. You don't have to eat a late supper anymore just because you're going to get home late. With a cell phone, no matter where you are, you can call home and tell the kids to put the roast in the oven."

"That's what they make oven timers for."

"O.K. Bad example. But when the family has personal phones it makes keeping track of one another a whole lot easier."

"That's one thing I *really* can't understand. Family phone plans. All those commercials make it look as if the kids and the parents actually *want* to talk to each other. I ask you, did you ever know a teenager who really WANTED to stay in touch with his parents?"

"Well, what if Jason's team bus is coming back to the school early, and you can't get there to pick him up right away? He can call you to let you know, so the two of you can make other arrangements."

"No one knows how to wait for anything anymore, do they. As far as I'm concerned, doctors and ambulance drivers are still the only people important enough to actually *need* beepers and cell phones."

"Well, ex-*cUse* me for living in the present."

"I hear music playing. Is that coming from your purse?"

"It's my cell phone."

"Your phone plays a tune?"

"Yes, it plays a tune. I need to answer that. It might be my real-estate agent calling about the house offer we made."

"Don't mind me. I'll just sit here and finish my sandwich while you fry your brain cells with electromagnetic waves."

(Too bad, she's already on the phone, so she didn't hear me. No matter, I'll just leave a little note on her plate: 'Thelma, I had to get back to work. Since I can't talk to you right now, I'll let you pick up the check!')

Here I am, eating yet, ANOTHER Never!

Cell Phones.

From previous columns, you KNOW how I feel about those intrusive instruments of so-called "modern communication."

They're obnoxious. They disrupt Anna's recital, Dr. Jefferson's presentation, and a quiet dinner in a restaurant with your honey—along with every other conceivable group gathering you can possibly think of.

When someone's cell phone rings in the middle of a conversation, they make the person he's with feel less than insignificant when he stops talking with them to take the phone call (unless, of course, he happens to be a doctor or policeman or firefighter, for which I can understand the intrusion).

It's not bad enough that the rings of those first, repugnant cell phones weren't sufficiently irritating to set one's teeth on edge. Cell phone manufacturers had to go and add musical jangles of every conceivable kind to the cacophony.

Now you can hear anything from Beethoven to Sousa to Twinkle-Twinkle-Little-Star coming from the depths of someone's pocket or handbag.

I know, I'm sounding more negative than my usual, perky, Crackpot self—and for that I apologize profusely. HOWEVER, I had to preface what I'm about to say with all those pessimistic protestations. For you see, I've gone and done it.

I got a cell phone.

Can you believe it? Geeze, I can hardly believe it myself, but there it is—blinking at me, daring me to pick it up and call somebody. You know, this little gadget is quite the marvel. A mini-computer smaller than the palm of my hand. It not only holds phone numbers, recent calls and voice-mail messages, it will keep track of appointments, calculate restaurant tips, and tell me what time it is anywhere in the world!

And this one's just your simple, basic cell-phone—no additional bells and whistles like the superwammedon models.

Twenty years ago—other than the science-fiction aficionados and the computer geeks—who'd have thunk such a marvel possible?

All right, I can hear you. You're wondering why I did it.

I could say I caved in to the pressure from my family (who worry excessively when I travel alone), or the inconvenience of having to hunt for a telephone whenever I needed to make a phone call away from home.

After all, if a body wants to keep up with society (not to mention her grandchildren), she can only hold out against the forward march of progress for so long.

In the end, I really blame it on temporary insanity.

So, now I have to figure out how to handle this thing. It's really not that easy. I don't mean the programming and the setting up. I got past all that with little trouble.

It's stupid stuff like trying to remember to carry the blasted thing (what good does it do me, sitting back home on my desk) or figuring out when to recharge the battery.

If I wait until the bars on the battery symbol are down to one, then it won't recharge fully, and the battery will develop a memory. Eventually it will recharge less and less forcing me to buy a new battery.

But if I wait until that last bar disappears, the blasted thing gives me only a beep or two of warning, then shuts down, right in the middle of a conversation. I'm stuck until I get back home (or back in the truck) to plug in the crazy contraption.

You see the dilemma.

And I haven't even touched upon electromagnetic waves eating up brain cells (as if I had any of *those* to spare).

"TA, Ta, ta ta ta. Ta tum ta tum, ta tum..."

Excuse me. But I hear "Stars and Stripes Forever" coming from my purse. You don't mind if I take that, do you?...

FAMILY

Because I'm the mother and I said so, that's why!

"If your best friend jumped off the Empire State Building,
  would you jump too?"
"Your ears are so dirty you could grow potatoes in there."
"You're going to sit there till you clean up every bite."
"If you fall and break your leg, don't come running to me!"
"If you're going to keep crying like that, I'll have to give you
  something to cry about."
"I don't know how you can sleep in such a pigsty."
"If I've told you once, I've told you a hundred times... "

How many of those sayings did your mother repeat? And how many have escaped your own lips before you had the chance to think about it?

When the hassles of mothering bring us to our wits' end, these age-old sayings just pop right into our heads and out of our mouths, don't they? And we don't even think about them, because they're in the programming!

Did you notice how many of these maxims of motherhood focus on the negative aspects of parenting?

As mothers, it just comes naturally for us to dwell on what's wrong—on what behavior we want our children to avoid; on pointing out what's dangerous in this scary world—instead of affirming positive behavior in those we love the most.

As a result, we inadvertently provide the very building blocks that put up emotional walls between the generations.

You know the walls I'm talking about—the ones it gets easier and easier to hide our true selves behind, because it's too dangerous to let out our tender hearts and risk getting them trampled.

We hand down those same blasted bricks our mothers handed down to us—the ones their mothers gave to them, from their mothers and their grandmothers, and great-grandmothers, and great-great grandmothers...

43

And as each generation marches by, the emotional pain grows deeper and deeper, while those walls continue to grow higher and higher—unless someone, *somewhere* along the line deliberately chooses to do something to begin knocking those barriers down.

> *Those walls continue to grow higher and higher—unless someone, somewhere along the line deliberately chooses to do something to begin knocking those barriers down.*

I know whereof I speak. My daughter and I had constructed some hefty walls between us during her tumultuous growing-up years. And it took some drastic measures for us to begin the process of breaking them down.

In our case, it took a blizzard, combined with Emergency Level III road conditions and getting trapped in my little pickup truck for over six hours, for us to start taking down those bricks, one by one. (Yes, the very trip in which we ate dog biscuits!)

But by the time we arrived back home after our hair-raising ride, both of us had done a lot of healing and a little more growing, and we'd made a wonderful start at breaking down those age-old walls.

I'm living proof that it IS possible to make soul-to-soul contact with the people we care about the most and begin the process of breaking down the barriers that separate us.

That doesn't mean it's easy, by any stretch of the imagination. But if you want to break through badly enough, you'll find a way. Just don't be surprised if it happens in a more outrageous manner than you ever dreamed possible!

By the way, I now tell people that I'm absolutely certain God has a great sense of humor—because of all my kids, Sally's the one He ended up sending to live right next door to her mother!

The relationship we're forging surpasses anything I could ever have dreamed possible between two such hard-headed, strong-willed women.

"Dear God, I bet it is hard for you to love all of everybody in the whole world. There are only four people in our family, and I can never do it. Love Nan."

(From the book, *Children's Letters to God*, by Hample and Marshal.)

No two ways about it—the people in our lives under the heading of "Family" aren't always the easiest people to love. But those are the very relationships that give us most opportunity to grow.

"I'll treat you like an adult when you start acting like one."
"I can tell when you're lying."
"Because I have eyes in the back of my head, that's why!"
"As long as you live under my roof, you'll do as I say."
"You can make the rules when you have a house of your own."
"Don't walk away when I'm talking to you."
"March right back down here and go up those stairs without stomping your feet."
"You just wait until your father gets home!"

Take the risk. Break through those walls of "Mom-isms" and make soul-to-soul contact with the real person hiding behind the worn-out clichés.

An' tell her the Crackpot told you to do it!

For Daniel Thomas Conrad

When smiles and frowns light a newborn's dreams,
    what does he really see?
Do those smiles reflect the angel-glow
    of another reality?

Can he hear the voices of heaven
    echoing in his ear?
Does the feather touch of an angel
    cushion his landing here?

How long will the angel dust linger
    till its gleam begins to fade
From the innocent face of this baby,
    so perfect and wondrously made?

I wish he could talk so he'd tell me
    of the mysteries before birth.
What was it like 'ere he came here,
    before he descended to earth?

Will he give me a clue as he's sleeping?
    Can I find one in each of his sighs?
Will I hear the soft whisper of angels
    as a dream flickers his eyes?

So I write down these verses for Daniel,
    as I ponder the marvels of life.
I thank God for my very first grandson,
    for son Jimbo, and Suzanne, his wife.

And I'm grateful they've made me a grandma
    and shared their new little boy.
These first two weeks in his brand new life
    have given this grandma rare joy.

For the time that one spends with a newborn
    reveals wondrous treasures untold;
The wisdom of sages lies deep in his eyes,
    and the heart-song of heav'n in his soul.

Daniel Thomas, may God grant rich blessings,
    may He guide your steps from above.
May He help you enjoy this adventure called life,
    and keep you enfolded in love.

Perks of Grandparenthood

Love 'em, spoil 'em, then hand 'em back to mom!

I think I'm finally getting the hang of this "grandma" stuff.

Love 'em, spoil 'em, then hand 'em back to your own kids so you don't have to deal with the whining and crying when it's time to put them to bed.

I ask you, what could be more fun?

For the record, I've spent the better part of the past two weeks in the company of my little grandson, Daniel, which has given me the chance to regress a bit myself.

I'd forgotten what it felt like to sit and play with play dough and let my imagination run wild; I'd forgotten the wonder of getting down on hands and knees to watch a daddy-long-legs mosey across the lawn.

And what a hoot it's been to teach a 21-month old (who's just beginning to put simple sentences together) how to crow for the sheer fun of it, like Peter Pan of old!

Grandma perks—no doubt about it.

For a short time during this two-week grandson visit, I've had the boy all to myself for two, full days while his mom and dad took a mini-vacation—his mom's first night away from her firstborn.

I think Mom had a harder time with the separation than Daniel did, calling up countless times to check on things back home. Those of us who have one or more progeny climbing their legs while trying to get dinner on the table may relish an occasional break from all the mothering chores, but we know that you never stop worrying about your kids—no matter how old they get.

During those two days alone, Grandma and Daniel had a blast doing things I seldom had time to enjoy with my own toddlers many moons ago.

We went for walks, picking up sticks to wave and acorns to count. We splashed in the wading pool and sprayed water on Barnabas (his water-loving Golden Retriever). We squished play dough all over the kitchen table and dumped building blocks all over the living room floor. We spent hours rocking and reading story books.

And if we watched the animated movie *Dumbo* once, we watched it 27 times! (I'm sure I have the crazy thing memorized.)

Daniel also helped Grandma bake cookies—a messy proposition, to say the least. I had quite forgotten how *helpful* toddler hands can be in the kitchen.

But hey, when they want to help, you let 'em help, right?

Of course right! (Especially when it's not your own kitchen.)

Daniel helped to measure out peanut butter, insisted on cracking the eggs himself, dipped his own cup into the can of oatmeal, and had a blast throwing chocolate and butterscotch chips into the batter.

Whenever I'd turn off the mixer, he'd say, "Ag'in, ag'in!" So we'd turn it on "ag'in." (Probably the most thoroughly mixed batch of cookies I ever baked.)

The best part about the whole cookie-making experience was watching Daniel lick the beaters. I'm not certain, but I think it was the first time he'd ever had the opportunity to lick one completely clean—the kind of mess only a Grandma can love.

He had cookie batter spread all over himself and all over me, not to mention all over the counter, the chair, the cupboards and the kitchen floor!

(Don't worry, I cleaned it up after I put him down for a nap.)

Would I have let my own children make that kind of a mess?

Heavens no!

But that's half the fun of being—and having—a grandma. Parents don't have the time for such messy, undivided attention. Grandmas most certainly do!

> *Parents don't have the time for such messy, undivided attention. Grandmas most certainly do!*

Last night Daniel's folks came home, and I have to admit, I did feel relieved to see them walk in the door.

Now don't get me wrong, I enjoyed every minute of my Daniel time, but boy, am I ever POOPED!

Perhaps it's a good thing they do live nearly 500 miles away. I'm not sure I'd have the energy to live any closer!

Labor & Delivery '90's Style

It's a girl... and it's party time!

Correct me if I'm wrong, but I always understood that, even though the whole birth process rates right up there as one of life's peak experiences, it also falls under the category of "private family affair"—at least, it used to.

In today's enlightened medical climate, it would appear that this whole birthing event has become a group activity.

Enter experience in point: as fate (and my youngest daughter's wishes) would have it, I had the opportunity to participate in the birth of my first granddaughter on the Ides of March.

But first let me state that I'm among the loudest to applaud the changing attitudes of medical professionals who have ushered in this more "relaxed" labor and delivery atmosphere.

Thirty-odd years ago, as I gave birth for the first time in the sterile, stainless-steel environment of an Air Force hospital over 2,000 miles away from all family support, I was lucky to see my sailor-husband for 15 minutes of every hour during my travail.

And heaven forbid that he be allowed in the delivery room, of all places!

(During the height of those Vietnam days, the prevailing train of thought from those in military command went something like this: "if we wanted you to have a wife and family, we'd have issued them in your sea bag," [which gives you a little peek into the kind of care the dependents of those soldiers and sailors received at the hands of so-called military doctors.])

To an inexperienced country-girl, fresh from the farm (and before the days of birthing classes, I might add) I went into that first childbearing experience quite knowledgeable

Daddy always told me there was nothing to it: "just like an old sow poppin' out pigs!"

in the logistics of animal births, but totally ignorant of what a female person would have to face in bringing her new little bundle into this world.

After all, my daddy always told me there was nothing to it: "just like an old sow poppin' out pigs!"

Only when I got three-quarters of the way through that delivery experience did I realize that I SHOULD have solicited my mother's perspective on childbirth!

Today, not only does the father participate during the entire labor and delivery process—coaching his wife's breathing techniques through each contraction, playing cards or games in between pains to background music of the couple's choosing (in this case a cello concerto), and finally cutting the umbilical cord at the appropriate moment—he can even camp out in the mother's hospital room until he takes his new little family home!

Talk about a 180-degree change in attitudes. (You can add changing semantics to that viewpoint, as well: no longer is it simply the mother who's expecting, now the "couple" is pregnant [even though the wife, alone, must still do all the real work].)

And when it comes to visiting hours these days, it would appear that practically anything goes. Sixteen months ago, at the birth of first-grandbaby Daniel, my daughter-in-law had no less than 27 visitors call at her birthing room.

"Congratulations! I just saw Little Lizzy in the nursery! She's a beautiful little girl," says the tenth person to enter my daughter's room not one hour after the climax of this day's labor.

"Thank you, thanks very much. Thank you eversomuch!"

"So tell me all about it! How *was* it?"

"It was awesome! Totally awesome! You wouldn't believe the effort it took to push that little bundle into this world…

…but maybe you'd better wait and ask the new mother what SHE thought of the whole ordeal… after she wakes up!"

(Welcome to the world, Elizabeth Ann Zink! We love you already!)

52

Changes in the 'Baby Business'
or
Nothing grounds you like a newborn

Tell me, did we have to haul around so much "stuff" when we raised our babies?

For the past week, with the presence of my daughter and newborn "Little Lizzie" with me here in Horsetail Hollow (while Lizzie's Daddy is away in Honduras), I've found myself regressing to the memories of my own baby-raising years on more than one occasion.

Now I realize that every new generation brings changes not only in the philosophy of raising its children but in the "stuff" it deems necessary in order to do that job "properly."

Take, for example, baby beds: my daughter tells me that these days "powers that be" require the bed slats in a baby's crib be no farther apart than the diameter of a Pepsi can (or Dr. Pepper, or Sprite—pick any can, they all measure pretty much the same.)

If the Crib Patrol should happen to come in and find that your baby's bed slats measure an inch wider than the aforementioned specifications, then you run the risk of having your baby confiscated.

They think it's true! Honest to Pete!

I shudder to think what the Diaper Deputies would have done to me, had they discovered that I lay my first, newborn babe to sleep in a cardboard box.

That heirloom crib handed down through three or four generations of tots will simply no longer do. (How in the world did all those previous generations survive, if that crib was such a terrible threat, I ask you?)

Or take a look at diapers as another example: I went to buy my daughter a package of disposable diapers, and I stood in that aisle for a full 15 minutes trying to decide which diapers to purchase. Oh, I narrowed down the correct size quickly enough.

> *How in the world did all those previous generations survive, if that crib was such a terrible threat, I ask you?*

But what IS the real difference between Luvs® or Huggies® or Pampers® or the generic brand, of diaper anyway?

I never had to worry about such things with my babies. One diaper did it all: fold it one way for newborns, another way for crawling babes, yet another for tots. Simple! Then throw it in the washer and use it all over again—earth-friendly; no conservation issues raised at all.

(Hey, you don't suppose that 10,000 years from now our garbage dumps will yield priceless, pressure-packed gems that began with all those buried diapers, do you?)

Car seats bring another interesting twist into the whole baby-raising equation. While I applaud the concern behind regulations governing the transport of little people—airbag issues aside—I think the whole "leave-them-screaming-but-firmly-strapped-in-the-back-seat-while-the-car-is-running" mode of thought carries things a bit too far.

How many mothers do you know who can keep their entire focus on the road when that baby's expanding lungs threaten to rival the decibel level of a of a jet throttling up for takeoff?

Again, the Baby Police would arrest me in a heartbeat today, cuz I not only put my babies in the front seat where they could see that their mother sat near enough to touch and reassure, but I also made use of that self-same cardboard box for newborn-transport purposes!

See, you don't need really *need* fancy folding-beds, super-wammedon car-seats or designer disposable-diapers to raise up a baby—they're merely statements of today's litigation-happy society. All you really NEED is a cardboard box and a dozen or so old-fashioned diapers. Simple!

(But, who would buy all this "stuff" if someone, somewhere hadn't made it appear to be so in-dispensable?)

I say raising a baby doesn't have to be as complicated as this modern world would make it look. Stick to the basics and your gut instincts; they won't lead you too far wrong.

> *All you really NEED is a cardboard box and a dozen or so old-fashioned diapers!*

Besides, nothing else I know gets you in touch with the real basics of life quite like the needs of a newborn baby.

I have to tell you I've loved every spoil-the-grand-kid minute of having Little Lizzie here. But I need to be honest, too: I like being able to have all the fun, then when I get too tired, just hand her back to her mama!

Welcome to earth, tiny Tessa Rose!

It's official. Tessa Rose Conrad, who couldn't wait to get here, made her grand entrance on this terrestrial sphere three and one-half weeks early—bestowing "grandmotherhood" upon me for the third time.

Since I qualify as the only grandparent with a "portable job," when the call to report for newborn duty came, I loaded up my computer and hustled myself down to Elizabethton, TN, to welcome little Tessa Rose—and to help ride herd on her nearly two-year-old brother, Daniel.

You know, I think I'm finally mastering this "Grandma" business, in spite of the fact that I had a bit of difficulty conforming to the job description when little Daniel made me a Grandma for the first time.

Love 'em, spoil 'em, then head for home!

I think I'm beginning to LIKE this job. And now, with another granddaughter to spoil, it's becoming more fun than ever.

Tessa Rose weighed in at just a bit more than a 5-lb. sack of sugar, and, as tiny-sized newborns often do at first, she turned a shade of yellow from a slight touch of jaundice, till all her bodily functions kicked in the way they should.

But thanks to home health services of Eastern Tennessee, and the use of a snazzy apparatus called a "Bili-Blanket," she returned to a healthy baby pink in a matter of days.

What an ingenious device, that! It employed the use of fiber optics to funnel the ultraviolet light from an attached box through a tail of sorts, into a little pad upon which the baby lay.

No heat lamps, no eye patches, no danger of burns—just a slick little vest which attached that pad of fibers to her backside, where the UV rays worked their wizardry to help her body dispose of the toxins built up from a not-yet-fully-functioning liver system.

When we got her all trussed up in said vest and flipped the switch—Voila! She glowed!

Hence she earned the nickname of little "Glow Worm."

When we got her all trussed up in said vest and flipped the switch— Voila! She glowed!

Now you realize, that big brother was not about to be outdone by this brand new sibling. Even though his parents did an admirable job of preparing him for this addition to the family, it behooved us to keep a close eye on him, nonetheless.

Daniel tended to get a bit rough when it came to "helping" with his new, baby sister (throw in the blanket, throw in the binkie, dump Kool Aide® on her head cuz she's thirsty). So 'Brraa-mma' did her best to keep him otherwise occupied.

Of course, Daniel did his part in keeping Brraamma on her toes for the entire visit, too. (I'd forgotten just how BUSY a two-year-old can be!)

Well, to make a long story short, after cooking and cleaning and generally keeping the Conrad "home fires burning" for ten days, this Brraamma's POOPED!

I have to say that I am eternally grateful I got the chance to be a stay-at-home Mom in order to raise my own babies, but I must also admit, I'm glad that I *don't* have to raise my grandbabies! Much as I love them, I no longer feel as if I possess the energy— nor the patience—to shoulder the full responsibility of long-term, child-rearing tasks again.

Love 'em, spoil 'em, then head for home!

(What a great concept. I'm glad I thought of it!)

Smile pretty and say, 'Cheese'!

Throw a two-year-old talker, a one-year-old wiggler, and a ten-month old, bug-eyed baby together with an inept, apathetic Wal-Mart photographer, and I can guarantee a recipe for chaos.

Enter aforementioned trio of youngsters.

You see, my daughter and daughter-in-law wanted a formal photo of all three grandbabies to commemorate this rare visit. These long-distance cousins seldom have the opportunity to see one another, let alone play together in the company of their grandma for a few days, so this time together was a big deal.

Having said that (along with mentioning the fact that this lame-brained grandma forgot to take along her camera to record this historic visit), we decided to head to the nearest Wal-Mart to take advantage of their superwammedon photo special.

Now if you've ever had occasion to tend babies or toddlers, you know that just getting three children cleaned up, slicked down and buffed to a shine requires a massive amount of energy, let alone trying to keep them that way long enough to obtain photographic evidence.

> *You know that just getting three children cleaned up, slicked down and buffed to a shine requires a massive amount of energy...*

Add going somewhere to that equation, and there's no doubt you'll have to change at least one of them (if not all three) before you reach your destination—especially since the youngest one's a spitter.

Now enter indifferent picture-taker.

Granted, not everyone has the temperament to photograph children, but you'd think someone paid to *do* such a job could at least manufacture a smile for them, wouldn't you?

We overlooked the fact that she stood back and ignored us, as we tried to place the kids on the carpeted stand in front of the massive, computerized camera. (That camera alone was enough to intimidate Lizzie, causing her to cling to her mama in fright.)

And we overlooked the fact that, once we finally got those wiggly children up there, she told us, "Oh, I can't photograph them that way. They all have to face the same direction, or the picture won't turn out."

(Right. Me thinks whoever trained this inept image-maker must have given her only one formula for setting up a photo.)

I have to admit, as one who has had a *smidgen* of experience wielding a camera in my job as a feature writer, I do have somewhat of an eye for setting up a picture. Her statement couldn't have been farther from the truth.

It came down to this: She had absolutely no desire to put forth the effort to help create a memorable photo for her paying clients. O.K., I hear you. So what can a body really expect for $5.95? (At the very least, courtesy, not to mention an *attempt* at a smile?)

You'll be happy to learn that we did manage to capture an acceptable photograph of all three children. And (to give our photographer the benefit of the doubt), she did finally crack a smile when we completed our task.

But perhaps she couldn't help herself. Maybe that dyed-in-the-wool, Tennessee gal just couldn't stomach these blasted Yankees who mobbed her work station just as she was about to finish her shift. Or perhaps her shoes pinched her toes so tightly that to produce any kind of smile was simply beyond her. Whatever the reason, I have to say that I am glad we finally got that photo.

And whenever I look at frightened Lizzie and bug-eyed Tessa Rose, I'll have to smile, as I recollect our little ordeal.

But the one thing I'll remember most about our photo project was hearing two-year-old Daniel say, "Chayeeese," with his little southern-boy, Tennessee accent!

Welcome to the world, Baby Gwyn!

When your mama made her grand entrance into this world, she gave one, loud squall, then opened her wide, blue eyes to bask in the glow of the spotlight.

It seems fitting that she ended up meeting your daddy and making her living by performing in the spotlight, as well.

Naturally, when you decided to join them on this July 19th recently past, I expected nothing less than a little Hollenbach who would also feel right at home under similar luminescence. The fact that you, too, spent your first hours staring into the lights, bodes well for your future as the daughter of a traveling, music-ministry team.

I must say, the fact that you turned out to be Gwyneth Grace rather than the little boy we all felt sure was coming, gave every-one quite a surprise—except, of course, for your great grandpa. However, I do believe that in her heart of hearts, your mama knew all along it was you.

And you couldn't have come to a more loving and devoted set of parents, little Gwyn. But I have to warn you, you'll need to learn the ropes of living a "life on the road" quite early.

You'll be happy to know that you already have a tambourine waiting for you, courtesy of a grandma who long ago saw you standing up there, with your mommy and daddy (better known as *Grant and Sally Ministries*), "Praising God, from Whom all bles-sings flow,"—and counting yourself first among those heavenly blessings.

I should also mention that it seems quite fitting that you bear a striking resemblance to your great Aunt Sandy, who (as fate and the good Lord's plan would have it), helped to ease your mama's travail as you made your grand entrance onto this terrestrial sphere.

Since I had the great gift of witnessing your delivery first hand, Little Gwyn, I can attest to the fact that your mama had the very best of care during the hours she labored to bring you forth, thanks to the skill and experience of my favorite (and only!) sister.

(Too bad you hadn't earned your nurse's hat, back when I gave birth, Sis. I can't imagine a more secure feeling than depending on the skill of someone you love, to see you through the great upheaval of childbirth.)

Gwyneth Grace—God's blessing—you have also come to an extended family that not only shares an abundance of love, but one that never lets an opportunity pass by to sing their praises to the Lord of the universe, Who has already blessed them all richly.

But, as your great Uncle Jim also says—"the nut never falls very far from the tree," so be forewarned, little blessing: the family you've decided to join possesses a quirky sense of humor, too. (I'm sure you already knew that, or you would have never given us such a birth surprise.)

So, welcome to the world, baby Gwyn! I promise I'll do my best to teach you all those things a grandma's obliged to impart to her grandchildren—how to watch butterflies and make mud pies, to blow dandelion fluff and search for fairy footprints.

I'm sure we'll discover many more adventures, during the time we have to travel together along this life-path. God grant that it be a long, long road, before we come to its end.

While the Cat's away, the mouse will play!

Attention grandbabies! Mommy and Daddy have flown the coop, leaving Grandma in full rein!

Well, in this particular case, we're talking one grandbaby, as Grant and Sally (of *Grant and Sally Ministries,* the dynamic Christian-music duo) record their newest album project down in Kentucky.

Here at home, Grandma and one-year-old Gwyneth Grace hold down the fort. Naturally, I received my detailed instruction list before Mom and Dad got out the door. Leaving a child in the care of another always comes hard for first-time parents, but it definitely strains the heart strings the first time they stay away from home overnight.

Of course, any mama worth her salt will err on the side of too many rules—especially when leaving her precious chick in the care of a Crackpot Grandma.

But before I can relate the hi-jinx afoot between Gwyneth and Grandma, I must backtrack a mite to fill you in on the tumultuous ride that another mother and daughter have taken over the years.

My Sally Ann began fighting with me long before she ever made her grand entrance under the spotlights of the delivery room at Wooster Community Hospital, while her daddy upheld his patriotic duty on an aircraft carrier off the coast of Vietnam. (She was six months old before he finally got to meet her.)

To say she demonstrated a stubborn mindset from the very start would come as a gross understatement. We butted heads from the very beginning, and we butted heads until she flew the coop. After that, we just kept our distance.

Low and behold, whom should I end up living beside all these years later, but my beautiful, talented, headstrong daughter.

(I always maintained that God has a mighty sense of humor; now I'm absolutely certain of that fact!)

Enter Gwyneth Grace, Sally's own introduction to motherhood.

Somehow, I think the souls must have gotten mixed up, up there between the generations, because Sally ended up with the most tractable, obedient, angel-of-a-baby I've ever seen.

Little Gwyneth Grace can win your heart with her first giggle, then seal it up tight when she blows you a goodbye kiss.

It hardly seems fair. The way I see it, in the grand scheme of things, Sally should have to deal with a bullheaded... I mean *determined* child of her own.

What ever happened to pay-back time?

O.K., I can deal with the fact that God sent her a sweetheart. After all, she's my grandchild, right? I can also thankfully report that Sally and I have broken down many of those emotional barriers that kept us at arm's length from one another for so long.

I can truly celebrate the great blessing she received in little Gwyneth Grace. However, as a grandma, I consider it my sacred duty to do what we grandmas are meant to do best—*spoil 'em*!

When I stay with Gwyneth at her house, dutifully, I stick to all "the rules" (well, most of them, anyway). But when Gwyneth comes over to MY house, we throw rules out the window.

When we play outdoors in between said houses, Gwyneth Grace makes up her own rules. That includes picking strawberries, eating dirt and studying ants and spiders up close.

Who knows, maybe before all's said and done, this little angel will turn into another great explorer who will accompany her Crackpot Grandma on many a great adventure.

We can but hope.

Meanwhile, we can leave her mama wondering what mischief we've been up to while she's away!

You finally made, Ethan Aaron!

What kind of dreams does a newborn dream
      when he lies there, fast asleep?
      Does he still hear the heart-song of angels
      serenading new souls in their keep?

Do his flickering eyes witness wonders
      too brilliant for grown-ups to see,
      as his two tiny fists clutch at whispers
      from a fading reality?

Can he yet feel the lifeline from heaven
      fading now, in the new dawn of birth?
      Does he smile at the angels who linger,
      making sure he lands firmly on earth?

Does he know that he sleeps on a cushion
      of selfless devotion and love?
      Can he sense that he's come to a haven
      abounding in gifts from above?

This fresh little spirit, now come to earth,
      Ethan Aaron, new grandson, new joy.
      May you glow with the sparkle of heaven,
      shining bright in your eyes, tiny boy.

May you always hear wing beats of angels
      while they hover protectively near,
      helping you grow strong and faithful and firm—
      wiping away every tear.

May you blossom through life's great adventure
      as the Lord guides your steps from above.
      May you master the lessons He brings you,
      as He keeps you enfolded in love.

Now sleep, tiny one, to soft lullabies,
and smile while the newborn dreams last.
Perhaps I can catch a small glimpse of heav'n
before all the stardust has past.

Welcome to the world, Schuyler Beth!

You'd think by the time grandchild number six made her grand appearance into the world, this grandma stuff might tend to become passé, wouldn't you?

Well, I'm here to tell you that it "just ain't so!"

Every newborn recreates the miracle all over again. From rosebud lips to tiny toes, the joy of holding a brand new life never grows old.

For you, Schuyler Beth, the blessings of this life have just begun.

You may not fully appreciate it yet, but you've landed in the arms of a most loving and devoted set of parents, Grant and Sally Hollenbach.

I have to warn you that learning to live the ropes of a "life on the road" will present itself quite early on, as the second daughter of a traveling, Christian Music-Ministry team, *Grant and Sally Ministries*.

I do *not* envy the challenges your parents face, now that they must cart two children (and their required paraphernalia) along with all that sound equipment everywhere they go.

Your unique presence will undoubtedly make itself felt in this music-ministry team quite early on. Granted, your mama has felt it for months already; now the rest of us get to enjoy that distinct pleasure, too.

Luckily, you already have a big sister, Gwyneth Grace, who's paved the way, so joining up with this team will most likely come a little easier for you than it did for her. I have a hunch, however, that it will *not* be any easier for your parents.

After gazing into those age-wizened eyes of yours, I'm certain that your parents are in for a wild ride. (I recognized the identical spark I saw in your mother's newborn eyes; there's no mistaking that force of personality.)

Although you may look a great deal like your big sister (as well as your great Aunt Sandy, who [as fate and the good Lord's plan would have it], helped your mama when you made your grand entrance here, too), I have no doubt that you will present your own, "force to be reckoned with."

Sooooooo, dear little Schuyler (pronounced *Sky*-ler [and we had quite the guessing game going here in Horsetail Hollow, trying to figure out that name ahead of time]), when you find yourself squelched and overwhelmed by all the necessary rules and regulations your parents are obliged to enforce, don't forget that you have an escape hatch right next door, over here at "Grandma's House."

Your big sister can show you the way.

Princess Buttercup—a brand, new life

Birth. No matter how many times a person has the good fortune to witness the entrance of a new life into this world, the miracle never loses its wonder.

My newest grandbaby, Ginger Elizabeth Conrad (but she'll always be Buttercup to me), made her grand entrance on January 26, in Elizabethton, Tennessee, and this grandma had the most unexpected gift of being a part of the whole birthin' experience.

To witness the grand *sploosh* of one grandchild entering this earthly sphere comes as a rare wonder. To have had all three of my children include me in one of their birth experiences (other than their own, of which I played not a minor part) is a true gift of the heart.

Little "Buttercup," not yet one day old as I write this, came as a welcome addition to the Conrad household. Big brother Daniel wanted to name this new baby "Sara," while big sister Tessa Rose had her heart set on "Princess Buttercup."

Mommy and Daddy had a different idea, however, and named the new baby after her maternal grandma, Ginger Rose.

Yet whether for good—or for comic relief—I fear this child will be stuck with Buttercup as a nickname for quite some time.

With a seven-year-old big brother to protect her, and a five-year-old sister to help Mama "mother" this new, little life, she'll need to learn to adapt to an active household in transition.

For you see, by the time she's no more than five months old, this family will pull up stakes here in Tennessee and move West to Spokane, Washington, where Moody Aviation is putting down new roots, and flight-instructor Daddy Conrad will embark on a new adventure in his aviation career.

Needless to say, little Buttercup will have to adapt to upheaval from the get-go.

That also means if this Crackpot grandma has any hope of seeing this child bloom and grow, I'll need to

Birth... the miracle never loses its wonder.

find a way to make the long, westward trek myself, as often as possible.

At least until July I can make the one-day drive to Tennessee in the portable "Grandma Suite" (my little Toyota Motor home) to experience little Buttercup's first, few months of life.

Guess the ol' buggy will have to get tuned up for bigger and longer trips!

Westward Ho!

But for now, I'll have to get in as much lovin' and huggin' as I can, while the gettin's good!

I hope you can stand it, Buttercup, because with so many people who love you, you're going to get squeezed more than most.

Sleep now, while you have the chance, little one. You're in for one humdinger of a ride!

Elijah Mark—Grand Finalé

I've always contended that the last child to enter a family brings along all those left-over qualities of Mama's and Papa's genetic mix, so as not to let a single, hereditary characteristic go to waste.

And to say that character sticks out all over you, Elijah Mark, is obviously an understatement of graphic proportion!

I have no doubt the path laid out before you will prove to be a unique one, little man. Already your wit and determination have shown that you are a most exceptional child.

"You're so good at putting together those hard puzzles," I tell this last grandson of mine.

"I *am* good. Just watch me!" (He's way too stinkin' cute!)

The protracted attention span you already exhibit in one so young completely baffles me. It reminds me of my own boy at your age, your uncle Jim. His focus and determination have carried him far in this life.

Where will such strength of purpose ultimately carry you?

Only time will tell.

And time—that most precious of gifts, keeps marching along for all of us. Already so many of your grandmas and grandpas, the predecessors whose genetic gifts now flow through you, have passed into the next world of discovery and adventure.

We can only guess what discoveries and adventures you will manage to find for yourself, during your journey on this terrestrial sphere.

Would that I could stay here to witness every one of them, but I realize that as my own time draws ever shorter, you will, of necessity, go on in this life here without me.

Know that no matter where this incredible journey takes you, Elijah Mark, you will always carry a part of me with you.

For, as your great uncles say, *"The nut doesn't fall very far from the tree!"*

Take this bit of advice from your Crackpot Grandma: relish every single moment this magical gift of life offers you. Experience all that you can—*everything!* For all too quickly, you'll come to the other end, looking forward to what comes next...

...and (if I have anything to say about it), you can be sure I'll be there waiting for you when you get to the jumping-off place!

Tribute to my Rapscallion of a Father

I grew up listening to your stories, as we gathered 'round the supper table, so I suppose it was only natural that in time, I would become a story-teller myself.

Since I always got in trouble for playing in the gravy dish and wrestling with Jim over who had the most room on the back bench, you probably didn't think I was even listening. But I did. And I learned a great deal about the giant of a man I called my Daddy.

As a very little girl, I enjoyed nothing better than riding on the tractor with you, often falling asleep standing up in that roped-off spot on the big Case—and even falling off, on one occasion, when I looked down to watch the world go by.

(The fact that I landed on my head probably explains a lot to many folks today!)

Since I spent more time in the barn and fields with you, than I did in the house with Mom, I came to love and appreciate the earth and her seasons by watching you plant and sow, by helping you tend and reap.

You taught me the value of good, hard work and the importance of staying close to the land. And you gave me a real devotion to, and appreciation for the animals.

You also taught me the importance of learning how to lose, and I learned my share about it while trying to raise a flock of sickly sheep. Over the years, and through my many losses, that lesson has come to serve me well.

When you gave me that first, Marine Band harmonica, you also gave me the thrill of creating my own music, which set the pattern for music appreciation at many levels throughout my life.

I can remember standing over the kitchen register for hours, playing "Here Comes the Bride" until I learned the position of all those reeds by heart.

Thank you (and Mom, too) for putting up with all the racket. I cherish the memory of sitting on the back porch of an evening, playing the harmonica along with my Dad.

On summer nights Sandy and I would lie in bed, listening to the putt, putt of your John Deere tractor as you cultivated corn— listening to you whistling and yodeling in the darkness—and we'd fall asleep, content that our world felt secure.

During the winter, when you spent more time in the house after our bedtime, thank you for letting us sing a while before you'd holler up the steps, "Quiet down and go to sleep up there!" (Sandy and I had our troubles getting along as we grew up, but one thing we could always do without fighting was to sing.)

Thanks for pretending you didn't hear us when we'd sneak down the steps and try to hide behind the sofa so we could watch the Lennon Sisters on the Lawrence Welk Show after bed time.

And thanks for letting all four of us pile into one bed when we got scared at night (I know we must have made a lot of noise, getting John tucked in between Sandy and I, and Jim all wrapped up in the bedspread at the foot of the bed—especially when we giggled so much getting John to say pasketti, skabetti, spaghetti!.)

Thank you for a childhood full of happy memories.

I have many other little-girl memories of spending time with you, Dad—some wonderful, some scary, but always full of love, no matter how loudly you may have blustered at times.

It didn't take me long to realize that no matter how gruff and crusty you acted on the outside, on the inside you were really an ol' softy.

That's not to say I ever took your blustering lightly, mind you. Underneath your irascibility, I knew that no matter what, you always loved me.

As I grew, I can remember the first time I realized that my Daddy was not a god: I was in the third grade, and we were getting ready to go pick corn. (I used to ride in the flat-bed wagon and push ears out to the edges, away from the corn chute so we could make the wagon fuller. I don't imagine you really needed my help, but it made me feel important to think that you did.)

When we walked over to where you had the tractor parked, you tripped over a tree root sticking out from that old locust tree standing by the corn crib, and you fell down.

I was thunderstruck: my daddy fell down.

I knew that kids fell down all the time, but daddies? Never! After all, they knew everything, right?

Only then, when I finally allowed my father to become human in my eyes, did I begin to know him in a more comprehensive light. He had his quirks and his eccentricities; he had his integrity and his guile.

He was a man—with both good qualities and bad, like any other man—but more importantly, he was my father.

Thank you, Dad, for loving me unconditionally, for telling me that I can do anything I set my mind to, and for urging me to get back up every time I fall flat on my face.

I'm proud I can call you Dad.

Seasons of Motherhood: times of challenge and reward

Motherhood—the most rewarding and challenging venture this life has to offer. It's exhilarating and exhausting, comforting and disappointing, encouraging and frustrating—not to mention downright hard work!

Whether motherhood is, was, or will be a part of your life, we've all HAD mothers, so we can definitely identify with the seasons of motherhood.

First comes the brand **New Mother**—that time of life that brings bottles and diapers, binkies and bouncy chairs, not to mention all manner of baby *stuff* past generations never heard of.

The New Mother wonders: "Will I ever get to sleep through a whole night? How can one baby dirty so many clothes? Geeze, will I always smell like sour milk?"

In case you haven't noticed, it's very easy to lose yourself behind the baby and/or child who's always sitting on your lap or clinging to your legs.

Next come the **Mothers of Toddlers & Preschoolers**—what I like to call the "unguided missile stage"—when black marker covers the hallway walls and nothing is safe from being flushed.

The Mother of Preschoolers wonders: "Will they ever be able to dress themselves? Will we ever get through a whole meal without spilling something? Will they ever stop whining? Will I ever get to go to the bathroom in peace?"

Forget about full make-up and fancy hair-do's. She's lucky to get 10 minutes to shower, dress, do her hair *and* put on a face, before the kids need to be changed, because they've already managed to get their Sunday clothes all muddy.

When a mother *finally* sends her kids off to school, she's introduced to the time of measles and mumps, chicken-pox and flu, not to mention broken bones, concussions and emergency-room visits.

Mothers of School-age Kids wonder if they'll ever get past being the drill-sergeant—"Don't argue with me, just *do* it! Because I SAID SO, that's why!"

In the morning, you hit the floor running to pack lunches and get them off to school on time; after school you spend hours behind the wheel, shuttling kids to piano lessons, swim lessons, dance lessons, ball practice, ball games, tournament games. etc., etc.; at night, you drop into bed, after fighting to see that they got their homework done, and finally turn off that blasted TV (unless you were brave enough to cut off the plug in the first place!).

However, before you know it, those school-age kids have turned into (dare I say it?) TEENAGERS!

Mothers of Teenagers everywhere—God Bless You!

You must face clothes explosions, hair-spray-covered mirrors and spilled nail-polish, as well as pop cans, pizza cartons and potato-chip bags all over the place. You're also likely to find greasy car parts in the kitchen sink and a whole gang of hungry boys raiding your refrigerator.

Did you think you didn't get to sleep much when they were little? Now you *really* get no sleep, because they're *driving and dating*!

Mothers of Teens now wish they were back to shuttling their own kids everywhere, because at least then you'd KNOW where they are: "Where are you going? Who's going with you? When will you be home? What time did you get home? What did you do? Who was with you? Good grief, You did *WHAT*?"

If you survive the teen and college years and are lucky enough to see your children married and on their own, Congratulations! You've finally worked yourself out of a job as Mother.

Now comes the fun part—being a **Grandma!**

You can finally get lazy and eat Stouffer's frozen entrées or eat ice cream for your own supper, because no one's gonna snitch on you. And you HAVE to keep plenty of cookies and candy around in case the grandkids come to visit, now don't you?

"But when *are* those kids of mine ever going to bring my grandbabies over?" Of course, when they do come, you end up cooking for an army, and you're back to cleaning up spilled milk and toddler messes under the dining-room table again. "Good grief, when are these people going to leave and take these wild children back home with them?"

Those who make it to the grand stage of **Great Grandma** definitely have reaped the Creator's blessings. Of course, by then it's hard to remember who all these children are running around here!

"How can all these people be related to me when I don't even know their names? I'm not sure I remember my *own* children's names half the time, let alone remember if I took my pills this morning!" Weren't my children just babies a few years ago?"

Where *did* all the time go? Why didn't I just ignore all the work and play with my family more?

> *The cleaning and scrubbing will wait till tomorrow,*
> *for children grow up, I've learned to my sorrow.*
> *So quiet down, cobwebs. Dust go to sleep.*
> *I'm rocking my baby and babies don't keep.*

The Tie That Binds

Do you gather for family reunions? Memorial Day weekend marks the traditional time our family renewed its tie and gathered for that first official picnic of the season.

For quite a number of years, our tradition had faded into oblivion as the generations expanded and spread apart. But a short while back, some of the younger generation decided to resurrect our family reunions of yore.

We wanted our children to have a taste of the fun we'd had so many years before. In the process, we rediscovered a rich treasure —our extended family.

When I was little, making a trek to the family reunion at my Dad's "old home place" was a time of high excitement and frolic for all the aunts and uncles and cousins who never saw one another very often.

Mothers would gather around the food tables Grandma had covered with oilcloth, arranging and fussing with baked beans, potato salad, and chicken & noodles we'd gorge on all day long.

And fathers would sit with Grandpa under the big elm tree, chewing over hog pedigrees, tractor repairs and cultivation techniques, while the kids ran circles around everyone.

We cousins would play Red Rover and hide-and-seek, or Johnny-can't-cross-my-ocean. And we'd climb trees or play under the "big stone," and then we'd play pyramid.

The biggest, strongest cousins (shoulder-to-shoulder on their hands and knees) always took places on the bottom. Then the middle-sized cousins would climb on top of them (all the while placing knees and elbows in strategic spots as we climbed on, trying to make them fall over).

If we managed to stay up past that point, the youngest, lightest kids among us tried to climb up both layers of shoulders and perch on top of the pile.

Ta-da!

Then we'd all collapse in a heap of tickling giggles, eager to try it all over again until the grownups called us to dinner.

We'd race to the washtub full of pop bottles cooling on ice and choose our favorite flavors, or we'd have glassfuls of lemonade from the big pitcher, then we'd make our way down the long table of food and fill our plates up with desserts—if we could get away with it, that is.

Invariably, our moms would catch us and send us back to get "real food" before we could stuff ourselves with goodies.

"Great chicken, Grandma." "Who made that elderberry pie?" "Could I have the recipe for those cookies?" "Pass some more of that watermelon down here, would you?"

With stomachs filled, dishes cleared away and babies put down to nap, fathers would walk over the fields to survey how much the corn had grown, while mothers took their turn to sit in the shade of the old elm tree. As they escaped the hot afternoon sun they'd talk of the latest weddings, the newest babies, and compare notes on raising children (and husbands).

The older kids would pester the "big boys" until they'd get a baseball game going over in the side yard, next to the woods, and someone would invariably knock a ball down the hill and make the smallest kids (who'd escaped naps) run after it—through the poison ivy, of course.

Years later at our first *re*-reunion, the same scenario played itself out all over—complete with a pyramid of giggling kids built from the newest generation of cousins.

Oh, the faces may have changed as one generation moved forward to fill the previous generation's spot in the lineup, but the more they all changed, the more they stayed the same.

> *Family trademarks recycle, one generation after another.*

Grandpa's ears showed up on a great-grandson. There's no mistaking those ears! And another cousin had Uncle George's walk down pat. And look, it's Grandma's hair on Aunt Louise! I swear I see Grandma's smile, too.

Family trademarks recycled, one generation after another.

The old elm tree may be long gone, and the dishpan full of iced pop bottles may have given way to Gatorade® and CountryTime®, but family tradition lives on.

"Who made that elderberry pie?" "Could I have the recipe for those cookies?" "Great chicken, Grandma." "Would somebody please pass that watermelon?"

SOAP BOX!

The Bumblebee Who Couldn't Fly

"All I can do is the best I can do,
and I'm doing the best that I can."

The first time I heard that little saying on the *Captain Kangaroo Show*, I never realized the impact it would come to have on my life.

Let me begin at the beginning.

I grew up with the Captain and his friends: Mr. Green Jeans, Mr. Moose and Bunny. When my own children came along, it tickled my heart to find that Captain Kangaroo still held his early-morning time-slot in the television schedule.

My kids and I would listen to stories about *Mike Mulligan and MaryAnn,* or the *Giant Jam Sandwich,* and we'd sing "Pickin' up paw paws, put 'em in your pocket," "I'm a little tea pot," and "Eating goober peas," right along with the Captain.

We never failed to laugh out loud whenever ping pong balls rained down on Mr. Moose, or when Bunny Rabbit tricked the Captain out of more carrots.

Happy memories, with positive, healthy messages to grow on.

Bob Keeshan's *Captain Kangaroo* premiered on **CBS** in 1955 and ran for 30 years before moving to public television for six more. During that time the show won six Emmy Awards and three Peabody Awards in its record-making run.

We unquestioningly ushered the mustachioed, grandfatherly Captain into our homes to educate and entertain in his gentle, loving way, as he wandered through his Treasure House shaking his large, ring of keys to the theme song we remember to this day.

Everybody trusted the Captain.

You didn't have to worry about bad language, unnecessary violence, or inappropriate advertising when The Captain entered your living room.

You could always count on Mr. Moose, telling his knock-knock jokes, Grandfather Clock, dozing peacefully over in the corner, and Mr. Green Jeans, who always brought along another one of his live, animal friends.

Captain Kangaroo taught us good manners, respect, and fair play. His relaxed manner and quiet morality made it easy for parents to trust him and for kids to love him.

Keeshan believed that children learn more in the first six years of life than at any other time. *"Play is the work of children. It's very serious stuff,"* he said. *"If it's properly structured in a developmental program, children can blossom."*

I've confessed it before, but I'll do it again: even after my young children had all started school and not a single preschooler remained at home to tune in The Captain, at 8 a.m. I'd turn on the TV set myself to usher that old, familiar friend into my living room.

Who could fathom a morning without a visit from Captain Kangaroo?

One particular story The Captain told came to mean more to me than any other: *The Bumblebee Who Couldn't Fly.* (I realize this may come across as terribly simplistic, but bear with me; there's a reason.)

Every day, that little bumblebee with a big, fat body and teeny-tiny, flightless wings walked two miles to the flower field, gathered his nectar, then walked the same two miles back to the hive. All the other bumblebees teased and taunted him, flying 20 or 30 trips for every one trip he made.

When they made fun of him, he always told them, *"All I can do is the best I can do, and I'm doing the best that I can."*

> *"All I can do is the best I can do, and I'm doing the best that I can."*

One day a big storm came up, and all the bumblebees' wings got so wet they could not fly. Grounded and terrified, they huddled together in the huge, scary, flower field and cried, because down there in the grass, they didn't know the way back to the hive.

Guess who should come along? You guessed it—that little bumblebee-who-couldn't-fly. Walking patiently home with his nectar buckets, he found them, panicky and soaked. "Not to worry," said he. "I know the way back. Just follow me."

He led the two-mile trek back to the hive and saved the day—not to mention his fellow bumblebees.

The moral? Doing your best may not *seem* like very much to someone else who might be capable of doing a whole lot more, but if it's the very best you can do, then that's all that really matters.

That's what the Captain said.

During the years I cared for a growing and energetic family I felt strapped to a constant treadmill of activity. You know the scenario—softball practice and music lessons, 4-H meetings and doctor's appointments, play practice, holiday get-togethers and school programs (along with a few emergency-room visits thrown in for added excitement).

After a series of emotional blows, physical setbacks, and several hospital visits, I found myself bedridden for a time and unable to care for my young family the way I thought I *should* be taking care of them.

Geeze, just the exertion of taking a shower left me shaking like a bowl full of Jell-O®.

I felt like a failure.

"What good can I possibly be to my family like this," I asked myself.

One day, as I lay on the couch, flipping through the TV channels looking for something to get me through the morning hours, while my body slowly recovered from a severe case of mononucleosis, I happened upon a rerun of Captain Kangaroo.

The Captain was familiar company, and at that low ebb of my life, I needed a positive, friendly companion. Guess what story he told that morning?

You guessed it: *The Bumblebee Who Couldn't Fly.*

From that day on, I stopped moaning about what I couldn't do and started being thankful for what I still *could* accomplish.

I kept trucking along like that little Bumblebee.

Slowly, over a number of years (and through a good many shattering setbacks), I began to regain the ground I'd lost. And eventually (if I keep on trucking long enough), I know that one day I will make it back to the hive.

Oh, I don't have any grandiose illusions about saving my fellow bees. But who knows? Maybe somewhere along the path, my little motto might give someone just the boost that's needed to "keep on keepin' on."

I know my kids will never forget that little bumblebee's saying. It hangs on my wall to this day as a constant reminder, because you see, *"All I can do is the best I can do, and I am doing the best that I can."*

Fourth of July—my personal Independence Day!

Break out the sparklers. It's the Fourth of July!

Perhaps I need explain the significance of Independence Day. You see, July Fourth marks a life-changing milestone for me.

It's my personal Independence Day.

Back in 1993 I made the heart-rending choice to live a positive life rather than be pulled further and further down the black hole of domestic violence. It was a decision that changed my life forever, and one that I've never regretted, no matter how grueling the road leading from that decision became along the way.

Abusive behavior respects no age barriers, no level of education, no socioeconomic boundaries. Those unhealthy habit patterns surface everywhere.

No matter how trapped you may feel, you don't have to put up with abusive behavior. YOU DO HAVE CHOICES.

The following questions can help you determine whether you are involved in a relationship that is, or has the potential of becoming, an abusive one:

- Does your partner: embarrass you in front of people? belittle your accomplishments? make you feel unworthy? criticize your sexual performance? constantly contradict him/herself to confuse you? do things for which you constantly make excuses to others, or to yourself?

- Does your partner: isolate you from any of the people you care most about? make you feel ashamed of them, or of yourself, much of the time? make you believe she/he's smarter than you, therefore more able to make decisions? make you feel it is you who are crazy? make you perform sexual acts that are demeaning to you? use intimidation to make you do what she/he wants?

- Does your partner: control the finances as a way of controlling you? make you believe you cannot exist without him/her? make you feel that there is no way out? treat you roughly, threaten verbally or with a weapon? hold you to keep you from leaving after an argument?

- Does your partner: often get extremely angry without apparent cause? lose control when intoxicated? physically force you to do what you do not want to do?

- Do you: compromise your feelings for the sake of peace? believe you can help your partner change if you can only change yourself in some way?

- Do you: find that *not* making him/her angry has become a major part of your life? do what your partner wants you to do out of fear, rather than what you want to do?

- Do you stay because you're afraid your partner might hurt you, him or herself, or the children, if you should leave?

If you said "yes" to ANY of these questions, you have identified an abusive relationship.

Don't hesitate to seek help.

If the abuse has occurred during the dating stage, don't count on marriage to "make things better." It will only get worse and eventually escalate into violence.

No matter how much you love someone, you cannot change the other person's behavior, but you do have the power to change yourself.

You don't have to live in a relationship of degradation and fear. You have the right to choose how you live, and plenty of help is available these days to do just that—whether it be learning healthy ways to deal with the relationship you're in, or helping you get out of one that's too far gone to save.

I intend no moral or religious overtones here at all. What you believe is your personal business. But what you DO becomes the law's business when it infringes upon someone else's health or safety.

> *In a healthy relationship, people nurture and support one another; they do not tear each other down or impose restrictions*

NO ONE deserves abuse.

In a healthy relationship, people nurture and support one another; they do not tear each other down or impose restrictions. You don't have to feel trapped, regardless of how helpless or worthless your partner has made you feel.

You don't have to let your children live in an atmosphere where they learn to feel helpless or hopeless, either.

You do have choices.

Choose life! Choose Independence of Spirit!

And break out the sparklers while you're at it, friend. They remind me that life bursts with surprises. In spite of the risks involved, the thrill of holding on to one still outweighs all the pain that appears to be raining down in its wake.

Have a happy Fourth of July!

Ask questions, expect answers, seek the truth.

Once upon a time there lived an inquisitive little girl who couldn't help but ask a lot of questions:

"What happens if I turn this handle?" (She'd get her fingers stuck in the wringer.)

"What will I see if I climb way up into that tree?" (A pretty nest, a bird's-eye view of the clouds, and a wasp nest!)

"What happens if I open up this gate?" (The cows would get out and she'd have to help her daddy chase them back in.)

"What will I see if I lean *way* over the back of this tractor seat to watch the ground go by?" (Stars—when she leaned back too far, fell off, and landed head first on the draw bar. [Good thing she had a hard head].)

I think you can see the kind of excitement that lay ahead for this little girl. She grew up a bit, and she kept right on asking more questions:

"Why do girls have to wear skirts? (This during the days of school-dictated dress codes.)

"Can I take my dolly to school?" (She would, until the teacher caught her making miniature English books for the doll, where it studied at a tiny desk she'd made inside her large one [she got bored waiting for the other kids to 'catch up'].)

"Why can't I climb the monkey bars and play baseball with the boys?" (Wearing a skirt did have obvious drawbacks; living in an era when "girls don't play Little League baseball" also put a distinct damper on the exuberance of her formative years.)

Like most children, the directive to "be a good girl and do as you're told" eventually ruled her outward behavior, but it didn't quench her questions. She kept right on asking—although now in a more "acceptable" manner.

About the same time she also learned something else: whole new worlds lay at her fingertips between the covers of a book.

Soooooo…

> the more she read, the more she learned;
> the more she learned, the more she knew;
> the more she knew, the more she forgot;
> the more she forgot, the less she knew,
> the less she knew, the more she read;
> and the more she read, the more she learned…

Beginning to think this might go on forever?? Good. Then like her, you're beginning to understand the real value of education. It should teach one to constantly question and search for answers. Because…

…the more you learn, the more you realize that you really don't know very much at all.

And if you're lucky, as you continue on the search for answers, you begin to realize that this quest for ultimate truth is really what keeps us all moving forward.

> *…the more you learn, the more you realize that you really don't know very much at all.*

Truth, you may ask… What *is* that? (I'm glad you asked that question.) I like to equate truth to the example of five blind men examining an elephant. (No doubt you've heard this illustration before, but it bears repeating.)

One man meticulously examines the elephant's trunk, saying truth is long, wrinkly and flexible, a little like a garden hose. Another man, examining a leg, says, "I agree it's wrinkly, but you're wrong about flexibility. Truth is thick and solid; it has six toes."

The next man says, "Wrinkly, thick, solid—yes. But only five toes, not six."

"I beg to disagree," says the fourth, holding on to an ear. "Truth is large, flat and waves back and forth in a swooping manner."

The fifth, holding on to the tail, says, "You're all dead wrong. Truth feels skinny and has wiry hairs at the end, and oh, my word, does it ever stink!"

Each blind man, describing his own portion of the elephant correctly, stuck doggedly to his interpretation of truth, and each one argued vehemently that the others were wrong. (You see where I'm going with this, no?)

Don't accept anything that *claims* to have the whole, total, absolute truth. Question everything. (Yes, even death and taxes—contrary to what you may have heard, neither is absolute.)

Listen to ALL the sources. Then glean the best from each in order to distill your own truth. I want to know what each blind man has to say, then, I not only want to examine that elephant for myself—I want to look him directly in the eye and ask him where he came from, where he's going, and how in the world he intends to get there!

Like Yentel of Jewish lore (who passed for a boy in order to attend school in a time when girls could not have a formal education), "I want more."

Encourage your children (or grandchildren, or nephews or nieces, or neighbors) to ASK questions and to SEEK answers. And don't ever, ever be responsible for squelching a child's God-given curiosity.

Who knows, he just might grow up and hold the answer to the question, "Why DO elephants never forget?"

Peaks & Valleys

From the aerial high of a blimp ride to the sobering depths of intensive care unit monitors, my life has spanned the full spectrum of life's extremes.

Funny, how both ends of the emotional gamut tend to counterbalance one another, isn't it?

When I climbed aboard the Goodyear Blimp, the thrill of taking such a ride made my heart skip a beat or two, yet short days later, my heart stuck in my throat as I stood watching life-support systems beep and pump in order to keep my closest cousin hovering this side of life's final door.

Why must we experience such extremes? Why *do* the peaks always seem to plummet into valleys? Do the emotional equations always have to balance out equally on both sides?

Now I don't claim to have any philosophical gift, but after living through a whole mountain range of emotional ascents and descents, I have come to realize that both extremes are necessary for life's landscape to have any character at all (and character, I've been told, sticks out all over me.)

The day I took the blimp ride, I'm sure my colleagues at the *Holmes County Bargain Hunter* showed great restraint in curbing their desire to stuff rags in my mouth or tie me to a chair as I bounced off the walls in anticipation of my adventure.

A few short years ago I would have swallowed all that excitement and showed a calm, cool exterior to my fellow workers. But I've finally come to understand the costly price for such repression.

When you keep building up all that pressure, sooner or later, the pot *will* crack, and I have the proof sitting right here on my desk—the Crackpot's cracked pot (which gives this book its name, by the way). Inner stress cracked that pot long after its final firing. I keep it as a reminder, for old habits do die hard.

Now, whether I'm whooping and bouncing off walls or crying my heart out on the shoulder of a friend, I'm finally learning to let myself *experience* my emotions rather than trying to cover them up or change them into some other "politically correct" response.

> I've finally come to understand the costly price for such repression... sooner or later, the pot will crack.

I've also come to understand something else: living the "abundant life" means experiencing the entire spectrum of human emotions.

As long as I can feel, I know that I am fully alive.

So, if you feel like jumping up and hollering *do it!* If you have an uncontrollable urge to break into tears (or song), let it all flow.

Sometimes, we have a hard time giving ourselves permission to do that, though, right?

If that's the case for you (as it still quite often is for me), just tell them the Crackpot told you to do it. And if anybody looks at you funny, tell them that it's "good medicine for the soul."

Consider the cardboard box

We all have 'em; we all use 'em—for packing away Christmas decorations or toting the cat to the vet. Maybe you have several jammed full of old National Geographic magazines you're not ready to part with yet, or "stuff to go through" before you organize the next garage sale.

When my kids were little, they looked at cardboard boxes and saw wonders. They became cars, trucks, airplanes, boats. Sometimes several lined up together would become a train or a tractor pulling a baler and wagon. (I raised my kids in the country, don't forget.) To the imagination of a child, the possibilities contained in a box were endless.

And what excitement when they got hold of a really BIG box! It could become a playhouse or a school building or just a neat hiding place where they might curl up with their favorite blankies to take a nap.

Sometimes I think the Grandmas could have saved themselves a lot of expense by eliminating the gifts altogether and just giving the kids a cardboard box!

(I may now be new at this Grandma game, but some lessons I have taken to heart.)

After watching my toddler and preschool grandbabies play during a recent visit, I got to thinking about an old picture I'd taken of my own babies in a cardboard box many, many moons ago.

Funny, but when I look at that picture, I don't recall the struggles or the pain or the lost sleep of those years. I remember the simple joy. My kids' infectious giggles over a new discovery had a way of smoothing over the roughest of life's bumps, just as the giggles of grandbabies now smooth over the sad reason for our family's gathering.

Death has a way of making one stop to mull over those important things we tend to let slide in our day-in, day-out, keep the-treadmill-running lives—like cardboard boxes and giggles of babies—and hope.

> *"Wonders never cease, if we never cease to wonder."*

I have a saying posted on my wall: *"Wonders never cease, if we never cease to wonder."* I guess that's a big part of the philosophy driving this "Crackpot" column—to point out what exciting and new things each cardboard box has to offer, if we just remember to look hard enough with the imagination.

Too often we "grownups" tend to lose that capacity for vision. (Hold on to your hats: here comes the sermon.)

I can get bogged down with all the problems and fail to see the possibilities those problems represent. When the septic tank backs up, and the roof springs a leak, and the lawn mower dies, it's not always easy to figure out how to make modest resources stretch to cover everything.

But even the stickiest (or stinky-est!) of situations offer rewarding challenges if I can just manage to see them in a more creative way.

I need only remind myself to look for the Cadillac in the cardboard box!

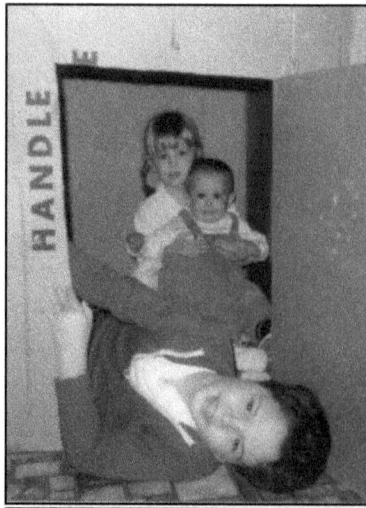

Find your own voice and sing your own song

You don't get harmony when everyone sings the same note.

Growing up in the heart of a Mennonite community in Wayne County, I had the advantage of hearing four-part harmonies ever since I was old enough to open my mouth and warble a tune.

And believe me, to those of us who spent our earliest, formative years in a congregation that sang nothing but a timid melody-line (with heads buried in hymnals to hide the yawns), any chance to escape the Sunday morning monotony and hear "real singing" came as a welcome diversion, when we'd visit a nearby Mennonite church.

Hey, to a kid who loved music, who really cared about the preachin'? I just wanted to raise my voice and SING! Now *that* felt like *REAL* worship—something you could throw your whole being into.

But (as any good girl who does as she's told soon finds out), proprietary concerns soon have a way of squelching individual notions to make a body conform to the dictums of "respectable society."

In other words, we're taught to do as everyone else does within our community circle—or risk the perilous consequences.

Yet, try as I might (and mind as I should) I couldn't get the message of that music out of my soul.

Listen to all those parts! Each one, taken alone, sounds aimless and ineffective by itself. But put it together with another part, and something wonderful begins to happen.

Add another part or two, and suddenly a broad, rich chorale sends up a blended symphony of song.

Amazing what the human voice can accomplish when it actually works together with other voices, singing their own, individual notes. Together they can produce a harmony that the single person never could hope to create alone (unless, of course, you can sing and whistle at the same time).

If you really want to hear something spine tingling and inspiring, start adding an instrument or two—or 10 or 20—until you have a whole orchestra of melodies and counter-melodies adding their unique contributions to the composition.

Handel knew it. Bach knew it. So did Tchaikovsky and Beethoven and all the greats.

Symphonic music is truly sustenance for the soul. (Scientific documentation has also proven that it makes plants grow faster, just in case you're interested.)

So what does all this singing business really mean, you ask?

Ever since my "wake-up-call" of late, the importance of "singing my own song" has taken on even greater meaning than it did before.

I'd failed to realize how often I slipped back into the habit of singing the melody line in order to appease those around me—or how often I've conformed to those unwritten "rules of conduct" just to avoid the kind of inharmonious discord that can set one's teeth on edge.

I'd forgotten the importance of singing my own song.

Native Americans believe that every person has his own, unique song and that a big part of our journey in this life is discovering its distinguishable sound.

I feel as if I've just begun to hear the haunting strains of my own, Crackpot song—and to realize the larger composition involved in its completion.

The work I've been put here—and left here—to accomplish demands that I pour my all effort into perfecting the harmonies of that individual song. And believe me, I still have a whole lot singing (and writing) to do before I belt out my last, little ditty.

I have no time to mince words and soften the discord, just to make everyone feel more comfortable while I try to get across my true meaning. You see, a big part of my purpose lies in making you feel "uncomfortable" by pointing up that very discord (while tempering it with just enough humor so it doesn't make your hair stand on end).

When we start to squirm in our seats—when we begin to feel ill at ease singing the same song everyone else does—only then can we begin to make the necessary changes that will transform the heart-song of our souls.

Life's too short to sing nothing but the melody.

Find your own voice and sing the song of your soul.

You are what you think!

You've heard the old saying "You are what you eat" (the basic tenet of which, no doubt, kicked off the whole health-food industry).

Well I believe another adage holds even more truth: "You are what you think."

What a person expects (or thinks) eventually does come to pass, you know. *Where your intention goes, your energy flows.*

Some would call that self-fulfilling prophecy, however I prefer to think of it as creating one's reality by the thoughts he chooses to entertain.

We can immerse ourselves in misery by constant negativity, or we can create a more optimistic existence by *choosing* to focus on positive thoughts.

For most of us with feet of clay, that's easier said than done.

If I asked you to give me examples of people who constantly spread pessimism and gloom, I'd bet you would rattle off quite a list. (You're probably even related to some of them!) But chances are you could count on one hand the number of cheerful souls who consistently leave sunshine in their wakes.

We all know negative curmudgeons who manage to put a black smudge on our spirits every time we brush up against them. It takes a lot of energy to be around such people.

On the other hand, those rare souls who possess an inner peace and manage to find the good in any situation bring welcome refreshment for the soul.

Of course we all *want* to be happy and optimistic. We *want* to see the positive attributes in any predicament. But when we're down here slogging through the mud, sometimes it gets awfully difficult to find a cleansing stream.

That's where the power of imagery can come in handy. Choose some positive image to focus upon, in which you can see your situation rectify itself. Then no matter what, HANG ON TO THAT PICTURE.

> *Where intention goes, energy flows.*

Without a doubt, you'll feel the temptation to flash back to those old, negative patterns so deeply ingrained. But whenever a destructive picture sneaks back up on you in an attempt to erase the positive one, push it back—holler at it if you must to chase it away—and MAKE yourself focus on the new, positive image.

That process can work miracles. I guarantee it.

So who am I to sit hear spouting all this power-of-positive-thinking stuff?

I'm just like you—an average person fighting the same kinds of battles to keep negativity at bay. It takes hard work to hang on to optimism in the midst of a pessimistic world (which is one reason I do not watch the evening news!)

However I do have first-hand experience with the power of this imaging stuff. I know the potential of holding fast to a promise.

Just ask my massotherapist. Ten years ago I had a severely curved spine, but today—thanks to her work on my muscles and my work at adjusting the thoughts in my head—I not only stand straighter, I'm a full inch taller!

You CAN change your life (or your waistline or your body mass or your reaction to a seemingly hopeless situation) IF you're willing to do the head work that's involved in making that change.

But if you think you can rely on someone else to do the work for you (or give you a magic potion to "make it all better"), then you're in for a mighty big disappointment.

It doesn't work that way.

Change has to come from the inside before it can manifest on the outside. (Now where have you heard that one before? Funny how that same message given 2,000 years ago still rings true!)

"So what does all this mean for me?" you may ask.

> *Change has to come
> from the inside
> before it can manifest
> on the outside*

It means that within you lies the key to finding your own "wholeness" (or as that same 2,000-year-old teacher put it: "the kingdom of God lies within you.")

Cancer surgeon Bernie Seigel says, "Listen to yourself, hear the sounds of your inner voices. Only then can you learn to sing your own song," (from his book *Peace, Love and Healing*).

What I'm really getting at here, is that the power of the mind and the soul is far greater than any super antibiotic the medical profession can pull from the black bag of its pharmacopoeia and much stronger than all the herbal wonders of the world.

To put it more bluntly—the power of the mind is a terrible and wondrous thing. So be careful what you think—because that's what you WILL become.

Is the glass half full, or half empty?

That proverbial glass: is it half full, or half empty?

Well, it all depends upon your point of view.

The same principle applies to any given character trait: each can come across quite differently, to people looking at the world from opposite sides of that selfsame glass—even to siblings raised in the same household.

One brother might say his father is a persistent soul, however, the other says he's downright stubborn.

To the first observer, his boss is a frugal manager, but the other one thinks he's just plain stingy.

Is your sister a spendthrift, or does she happen to show a generosity that few possess?

Is Uncle Melvin a clown, or does he just have a very good sense of humor? Is Aunt Minnie over emotional, or does she have the innate ability to empathize and feel another's pain?

Does Cousin Homer come across as a braggart, or is he simply an excellent salesman who has a winning way with words?

I think you see what I'm getting at. A shift in one's outlook can make all the difference in the world.

Yet, that shift does not come easily to the soul who has viewed the glass as half empty all his life—nor to the one who's spent his energy focusing not on the donut, but rather on the empty hole at its core (unless of course, it's a jelly donut, which changes everything).

I say, let's give the poor schmuck... I mean that cynical soul, the benefit of the doubt. Perhaps he has to examine things more carefully, weigh the pros and cons of a subject more thoroughly, before pronouncing that the glass is, indeed, half empty in his eyes.

Who can say?

> *I prefer to see roses, rather than thorns— to see rainbows instead of the rain.*

I've always tried to look at the half-full side of things, myself. I prefer to see roses, rather than thorns—to see rainbows instead of the rain.

That doesn't mean I'm oblivious to the thorns or the thunder. I know life can leave us bruised and battered at times—that we can end up bloodied and soaked to the skin.

We don't need to stay that way, however.

"Two men looked out from prison bars; one saw mud, the other saw stars."

I think the majority of people in this world would like to believe they see the stars in spite of the bars that hold them hostage.

Unfortunately, in the process of trying to extricate ourselves from those situations that keep us in bondage, we tend to get bogged down in the muck of life more often than any of us would care to admit

Life's too short to squander our time wallowing in the mire.

"Sooooooo," I ask, "what can I *DO* with all this mud while I'm down here?"

Well, what else do you think any self-respecting Crackpot would do? She'd shape it into a serviceable pot!

"Good grief," says friend Thelma. "I always knew you had a hole in your head."

"Go ahead and think 'hole in the head' if you like," I say with a smile. "I prefer to say that I'm 'open minded'."

"O.K., then, *open-minded* friend, tell me, do you see the glass half full or is it half empty?"

"As far as I'm concerned, it really doesn't matter. *Clearly,* there's room for more wine!"

Simplify! Simplify! Simplify!

Slow down and smell the roses!

How many times have you heard that mandate? And how many times have you told yourself, "Yes, I know I need to slow down, but I don't have time today. I'll have to do it tomorrow."

I've got news for you, friend. With that attitude, tomorrow never gets here.

Why not MAKE the time to take stock of your life right now?

Where, exactly, does all this busy-ness really take you? Are you happy with the pace you keep? Do you enjoy your life every day, or do you keep telling yourself: tomorrow, next week, next month or next year I'll have time to _____ (you fill in the blank with something you really want to do).

I have to tell you, as one who made the deliberate decision to slow down my own life, I haven't regretted stepping off the "punch-the-time-clock-to-keep-the-treadmill-running-world" for one minute, even though it does have its moments of uncertainty.

This *slowing down* and *taking stock* business can be frightening stuff. When you're used to constant activity, life in the slow lane can throw you for a loop. You see, we're so accustomed to having to *accomplish* something, to *being productive* every moment of every day, that it's downright scary to stop.

Simplicity and living deeply means shedding all the outward layers of image and busyness that keep us from being close to ourselves and vulnerable to other people.

It means not just throwing away the day planner and the carpool schedule, but living from your essence, from your core. And you can only discover this "core of being" when you slow down and make the decision to live deliberately.

> *...relish every moment of life with full awareness and passion*

For the essence of living simply means that you come to relish *every* moment of your life with full awareness and passion.

Welcome the pain and learn from it. Embrace the ecstasy and revel in its brief reprieve. Learn all you can from every experience and emotion life brings your way.

Sad to say, most of us choose to stay busy, busy, busy and avoid dealing with life at its essence, because we're afraid to discover who we really are. For when we slow down, we begin to actually see and feel those things our busyness has kept at bay.

We're forced to deal with the hurts we've swept under the carpet and kept trampled down by all the constant hubbub.

In "*The Simple Living Guide*" (a wonderful book I highly recommend, by the way), Janet Luhers says, *"We feel a need to be surrounded by people, by activity—anything but solitude. Solitude takes practice. It requires facing down loneliness and realizing there is nothing more important (than getting in touch with one's core) that you can do."*

Any step we take to get a handle on the tangible messes we make of our daily lives helps in setting some order to those intangible ones, too.

Do something now to make your life simpler, more organized, less complicated, less cluttered—even if it's as simple as cleaning out your closet or your dresser drawers (a great winter task).

Take a hard look at your marked-up calendar and begin to structure your time around the things that are really important in your life. The simple exercise of making deliberate choices in your daily activities will help you begin to feel a little more control in a hectic pace.

> *We are not human do-in's, you know; we're human be-in's.*

If you do nothing else, at least take ten minutes for yourself, alone—every day—just "to be." (We are not human *do-in's*, you know; we're human *be-in's*.)

Our bodies and souls require breathing space—especially in this crazy, fast-paced, digital world that whizzes around us every second of every day.

So be good to yourself this week. Make a little time to "be." If anybody asks you why you're not doing something, tell 'em you are—you're taking a "soul breather."

'Cuz, it takes time for our souls to catch up with our bodies.

So let the sunshine in...

Remember the days when mothers actually shooed their children outdoors to make them "stretch their muscles and soak up some fresh air and sunshine," instead of letting them vegetate in front of the TV?

I always thought my mother did that to get us out from under foot; now I know better.

Even though medical professionals continue to issue warnings about the detrimental effects of the sun's ultraviolet rays, I still believe that children need sunshine to grow strong, and we all need those soul-warming rays to stay healthy.

Consider these reports and see if you agree:

"Our bodies need the nourishment of the sun to create vitamin D, which increases calcium absorption and acts like a hormone to encourage bone remodeling," says an article from the Jan/Feb. issue of "A Real Life," by Barbara McNally.

"A new study on vitamin D shows that women who receive 200 IUs of vitamin D daily from sun exposure or diet have a 33% lower risk of breast cancer than those who receive less than 50 IUs a day... the study found that women who lived the longest in sunny regions or who had moderate to frequent sun exposure had the lowest risk of breast cancer."

That bit of information came from an article entitled "Vital Vitamin D," published in the Mar./April issue of "Herbs for Health." The data for that article came from The National Center of Health Statistics as part of the first Nutritional and Health Examination Survey.

Here's another interesting tidbit: "A study of patients at a Boston hospital found that more than half had too little vitamin D... a condition that increases the risk of bone fractures," says Daniel Q. Haney, Associated Press Medical Editor, in a March news article.

"Vitamin D deficiency is much more common than most people had anticipated (especially among seniors)," says Dr. Joel S. Finkelstein, co-author of a report published in a March issue of the New England Journal of Medicine.

"The body makes vitamin D naturally from exposure to sunlight, however people who stay inside a lot, especially in the winter, may not produce enough vitamin D to keep their bones healthy," added Finkelstein.

Have I convinced you yet? Not only do our bodies need sunshine, our mental well-being depends upon it. Countless news and magazine articles over the past several years attest to the reality of SAD (Seasonal Affective Disorder) which plagues people during the short-lighted months of winter.

Those living in extreme northern and southern latitudes (e.g. Alaska, New Zealand, etc.) feel the effects of short-lighted days much more acutely than the rest of us.

So my gut instincts haven't been that far off base, after all. We really do need sunshine!

But don't forget, there is a *sensible* way to go about soaking up those rays. Tender spring-time skin cannot stand unlimited exposure without suffering ill effects, you know.

It takes a little common sense to build up one's exposure to the sun—and the more sensitive that skin is to begin with, the more in the way of practical protection one must employ.

In other words, slather on some sunscreen when you plan to spend much time outdoors.

A healthy respect for the potential harm that the sun's rays can inflict is a sensible thing, but don't let fear of the sun turn you into an lily-white couch-potato, either.

Taken in reasonable doses, sunshine helps us stay healthy.

And it's just as important for older folks to soak up those rays, as it is for the youngsters. (So the next time your mommy tells you to go outdoors and play, don't argue! If you don't have a mommy to send you outside anymore, make sure you take yourself out there once in a while to enjoy the wonders of nature.)

Of course we could take this whole discussion into the realm of quantum physics, where people the likes of Albert Einstein and Richard Feynman spent a good deal of their lives trying to understand the nature of light.

Without going into the details of colliding photons and electrons and the role that electromagnetism plays in holding electrons in their orbits to form matter, suffice it to say that according to the physicists, we are *comprised* of light—FROZEN light.

("Thou has made him [man] a little lower than the angels [beings of light]," Psalm 8:5.)

Not only do our physical bodies require sunlight to stay healthy, so, too, do our spiritual ones. (You can spell that s-u-n-light or s-o-n-light, whichever you prefer.)

Is it any wonder that we seek the sun?

I guess that famous John Denver song pretty well sums up my philosophy: *"Sunshine on my shoulders makes me happy..."*

Why not soak up a few rays today and feed your soul?

TRAVEL AND ADVENTURE

Got the itch to travel? Scratch it & go!

If you could travel anywhere in the world, where would you like to go?

Down the Amazon? Up the Eiffel tower in Paris? Do you yearn for the land down-under to see kangaroos hopping in the Australia's outback? Or maybe you just want spend a few days visiting relatives in Pittsburgh.

Wherever you want to go, don't wait—do it!

If you think you have wait to take a trip until you get all the chores done, I've got news for you—you'll never make it out of the driveway.

"But we have to wait until the kids are old enough," you say, or "until we get the car paid off," or "until the last child has graduated from college before we can take that trip we've always dreamed about."

Whatever you do, DO NOT let the "until" virus keep you from doing something that you really want to do.

Remember the old adage: "where there's a will, there's a way."

When you set the ball in motion, it has a way of bouncing in the right direction.

Besides, you don't have to spend a lot of money to have a great time. And you can have fun with the kids, no matter what their ages—it just takes a little bit more planning to keep them all busy so you can enjoy the trip, too.

(By the time you have them find license plates from every state, spell out the alphabet from road signs, and sing "Found a peanut" 27 times, you will have arrived at your destination!)

Over the years of my various lifetimes, I've had the opportunity to travel quite extensively in this world of ours, and most of those treks have been taken on a pretty skimpy shoestring—especially during the "Navy years."

Can't afford to stay in hotels? Take along your tent and a sleeping bag and stop at campgrounds along your route. You'll meet some pretty interesting people who make camping the main reason for their travel.

Can't afford to eat in restaurants all the time? Take along plenty of snacks, and stop in at a neighborhood mini-mart for a loaf of bread and a pound of bologna to make sandwiches at the next scenic rest stop you come to.

Be sure to ask the checker about interesting places to see off the beaten path, too. Sometimes you'll stumble over the highlight of an entire trip completely by accident. Or you'll discover a "character to remember" who made the whole trip worthwhile.

> *I believe that people are generally about as friendly and helpful as you expect them to be.*

Don't be afraid to talk to people. Contrary to popular belief, they're not all "out to get you." I believe that people are generally about as friendly and helpful as you expect them to be.

If you look for trouble—that's exactly what you'll find. But if you enter into a conversation with a friendly smile and an open mind, you'll most likely come away from the encounter a much richer person.

When my daughter and I took a trip to Florida to see her grandmother a few years back, I had a grand total of $80 in my pocket to cover the entire expedition (and I had to sell some of my antiques to get that!).

I threw an air mattress in the back of my little pick-em-up truck, took along the hibachi and a cooler loaded with food, loaded up my trusty ol' Labrador Retriever, and away we went— off on a quest for adventure. We spent more than one night camping in the rain at a rest-stop, with my ol' Lab standing guard under the tail-gate.

And guess what? We made that meager amount stretch in such creative ways, we had a blast! My daughter still talks about that trip, although it was NOT the journey where we ended up eating dog biscuits. (Hey, they don't taste too bad, if you have nothing else at hand and you're REALLY hungry!)

Don't think you have that kind of adventuresome spirit in you? You'll never know for sure if you don't leave the familiar landscape of your own driveway, now, will you?

When you take the initiative to travel, you not only expand your horizons (quite literally and figuratively speaking), you also add immeasurably to the rich store of knowledge that we're in this life to gather.

And when you finally return from your pilgrimage, glad to feel the comfort of your own bed and to have a "good drink of water from your own well," you'll know that your vacation has accomplished its purpose...

...because no matter where you travel, and no matter how far you roam, your trip cannot be a resounding success till you feel that there's *no place like home*.

I can't believe I drove the whole thing!

Twenty-five-hundred miles, plus! And I drove every mile of the trip myself—to Ft. Myers, Fla., and back, that is.

Now, you'd think that for someone who's already stretched her wings to travel solo, half-way around the world to New Zealand, a trip to southern Florida on a family mission would feel like a short jaunt, no?

I can tell you, that when you're the one putting in the windshield time, those miles stretch a powerfully l-o-n-g way—especially the last two hours of flat, sandy, Florida heat in a vehicle that has nothing but 4/60 air conditioning (four windows down at 60 miles-an-hour).

Pushing my little Pontiac, "Eric-the-Red," up to the 70 mph mark, stretched him beyond the capacity of his aging transmission. Geeze, it just surprised me that he had the stamina left in him to make such a trip in the first place, let alone make it all the way back to Ohio!

Soooo, if you're a Crackpot traveling alone, in a not-so-reliable vehicle, how can you help but find adventure along the way?

Perhaps I should revise that statement: when you're a Crackpot traveling with only a dog for company (an excuse to stop and exercise at regular intervals), how can adventure not find you?

Enter "Rocky Road," alias "Roxie," my travelin' buddy. This Chocolate Lab/Dalmatian-mixed pup, who just passed the five-month-old mark, weighs in at about 50 pounds at the moment. She's still growing.

Now, anyone knows that a pup, regardless of size, has lots of energy. Stick one in a traveling kennel for 10 hours a day, three days in a row, and you have a live grenade on the end of a leash whenever you let that pup out of said kennel for the relief of necessary bodily functions.

Ever see the comic-strip dog, *Marmaduke,* who takes his master for a walk? Then no doubt you get the picture. At each rest stop we'd make (roughly at two-hour intervals), I got walked sufficiently not only to work out the kinks from my all-day driving marathons, I probably lost a good two pounds per walk, to boot!

Whenever I'd get too tired to drive any further in a day, Roxie and I would stop to make camp. I didn't let the fact that (as of yet) I have no RV nor tent to pitch, stop me from camping out, either. (Remember, you're talking to a Crackpot who's spent the best part of the past two years sleeping in a tipi—and no, I did not attempt to travel with the tipi this trip.)

We'd set up our camp out in the open, at State Parks along the way, and I'd stretch out in the back of my little station wagon to sleep each night. Hey, it felt pretty comfortable, considering I had a playful, 50-pound pup curled up right beside me. She's a big chicken, left outside by herself.

Besides, I didn't figure anyone would even think about messing with a lone woman crazy enough to travel and camp with a BIG dog. Nothing makes a better guard than a big, *scared* dog, either. Not a thing moved out there, that I didn't know about.

Hey, if I'm going to be a traveling, "RV-Grandma," then I'd better start getting in some practice and train my dog for this traveling life, right from the get-go. I'm gonna be ready when my RV finally finds me.

By the way, I did some looking at several RV dealers, during the time I spent down in Florida. Talk about sticker shock! (Methinks I'd better get another book or two in the works, post haste, and hope to land a publishing deal that includes a hefty advance on royalties.)

You'll be happy to know that I arrived back home without major incident. "Eric-the-Red" (bless his oil-leaking heart) perked along like a trooper. And Roxie (now nearly two inches taller and 10-pounds heavier) couldn't have been happier to reach a place where she *finally* escaped the strangle-hold of a leash.

And I do believe my left arm now measures three inches longer than my right!

New York, New York!

Times Square and Rockefeller Center. Radio City Music Hall and Greenwich Village. Central Park and St. Patrick's Cathedral. I got to see them all recently on a fabulous holiday trip to the sparkling Big Apple!

I must admit, life in the concrete jungle can come as quite a shock to a dyed-in-the-wool country girl like me, but after the first day and a half, I managed to get the "rules" down pat:

#1) Never look anyone straight in the eye.

#2) If (heaven forbid) you should happen to make direct eye contact with someone, do not by any means, smile! People look at you funny if you appear too happy.

#3) If you work up the courage to take a taxi, don't expect to hear any form of English you can decipher. You'll also need to be prepared to find your way back from wherever the cab driver ends up taking you (most likely not remotely close to where you intended to go.)

Take your ear plugs along, too, I don't think a soul can drive in New York City without blowing the horn—*repeatedly!*

#4) Which brings me to the subway: Should you elect to ride on the underground tubes, try to find a seat by a door (if you can), then for the rest of the trip pretend you're asleep while you hold on to your packages with a death grip.

#5) If you can't handle the uncertainty of riding subway or taking a taxi-cab, you'll have to walk wherever you need to go—unless you want to try the bus system (which is another adventure altogether).

You could take a limousine, but that's not an option for the average Joe, since most limos require a two-hour minimum.

I did get to ride in a limo one night, though—first time ever in such leather-lined luxury! Quite posh, to say the least. And that driver actually spoke English you could understand!

#6) When you do elect to walk around New York City, you must never appear to look at your surroundings nor enjoy the sights. Instead, put your head down and walk as fast as you can through the humongous crowds. (You can't walk in a straight line for all the people, either.)

#7) And while you walk, you must buy a soft pretzel from one of the many street vendors hawking their wares on every corner. They toast the salty-snacks over a charcoal fire in cast-off shopping carts, making the pretzels burnt to a crisp on the bottom, while they're ice-cold on top!

Needless to say, I didn't follow the rules very well. I gawked at everything, pointing up here and over there, smiling at people all around. They looked at me in horror, as if I'd lost my mind (course, the folks who know me swear I did that long ago).

I can't begin to recount everything we did on this fairy-tale trip, but to say that "Mr. Goodyear" and I had a ball, is an understatement.

From the top of the World Trade Center*, overlooking all of Manhattan and surrounds, to the guts of the city's underground subway system, I witnessed a kind of life I never dreamed I'd get to see, let alone experience.

We did go into one of the department stores, Sak's Fifth Avenue, and look at furs, just for the fun of it, but with a full-length sable coat ticketed at $135,000, I thought it just a bit too pricey for the pittance in mad-money I had burning a hole in my pocket!

Even though I enjoyed this New York adventure immensely, I must admit I felt relieved to see wide-open spaces and clean snow again.

Dorothy said it best, and I can't improve on her quote one bit—*"There's no place like home."*

(I bet she didn't find an electric shoe-polisher in her hotel room to shine-up those sparkly, ruby slippers before she returned from Oz, either!)

---

* This trip taken before the New York World Trade Center came down.

Airport Security

Beep! Beep! Beep!

"She set it off. O.K., Ma'am. Take everything out of your pockets," said the Los Angeles International Airport Security officer on duty at the entrance to the LAX international gates.

In case you didn't know, this Crackpot's on an adventure of global proportion that will take her to the southernmost tip of the south island of New Zealand in the trip of a lifetime.

I arrived at the Los Angeles Airport around noon California time, after leaving from Port Columbus at 9:30 a.m., on March 6, 2000. But my eight-hour layover in L.A. has not been wasted. I burned up a big chunk of that time just toting my luggage across two miles of terminal, standing in line at check-ins, and getting hung up in airport security!

As in those good ol' military days of yore, the name of the game in traveling circles is "hurry up and wait." You rush like crazy to get to the airport in time to make your flight, then what do you have to do but stand there in line and wait!

> ...the name of the game in traveling circles is "hurry up and wait."

Finally, comes my turn through security: as requested, I emptied the contents of my pockets, and I also removed my watch, necklace and silver hoop earrings, just to be sure this time. I'd set off the alarm back in Port Columbus, too, but they passed me through after scrutinizing my jewelry.

O.K., I'm ready to walk through the metal detector once more.

Beep! Beep! Beep!

"She set it off again. I'll have to 'wand' you now, Ma'am."

Oh-oh... the wand! Actually, you just have to stand there with arms spread, while the security officer waves a more powerful, hand-held, metal detector wand across your body, front and back.

Beep! Beep! Beep! This time the beeps center over my spine.

(Ah-ha! The light bulb finally comes on! My back brace! It has metal stays. I shouldda known.)

The good news is, they passed me on through without forcing me to disrobe and remove said back brace from my person. The bad news is, this thing is killing me! How in blazes did those Victorian women ever survive wearing corsets, I want to know!

Guess one of the concessions I have to make in order to tote my own luggage at this "mature" stage of life is accepting the acquisition of a few necessary helps—like this back brace and the nifty knee cuff for this trick knee, and the ankle brace for that weak ankle...

...Good grief, whatever made me think I could travel so far on my own in such a condition?

Solo travel does have its freeing advantages, but a few things —like guarding the luggage at the other end of the security check when you're held up at the metal detector—do present more of a challenge.

"Hey Buddy! You, over there by the security belt. That's my carry-on bag!"

Adventures in food, New Zealand style

Rice Bubbles or Weet Bix, roast mutton or *fish pie, Milo, Marmite, sultanas* and *lollies*—how many of those foods can you identify?

A good many of the edibles I've had the opportunity to sample here in New Zealand (as I visit at the Topham dairy farm at the southern tip of the south island of this ocean-bound country to the east of Australia), differ more in name than they do in actual identification or taste.

Take *Rice Bubbles*, for example: in the U.S. we call the same thing Rice Krispies. But *Weet Bix* is something altogether different. The Kiwis (New Zealanders) eat their Weet Bix as a hot or cold cereal, and it looks like a cross between our shredded wheat and a melba-toast-type biscuit, with a taste that falls somewhere in the middle.

Of course mutton explains itself, if you know anything at all about sheep. But even though we seldom see lamb or mutton trussed up at a U.S. meat counter, it's quite common here, where the sheep easily outnumber the people by at least ten to one.

By the way, roast leg of lamb served up hot with mint sauce tastes out of this world. The only thing better, in my humble opinion, has been the fish and egg pie: smoked salmon mixed with hard-boiled eggs, topped with mashed potatoes and grated cheese, served up bubbly from the oven—fabulous!

When it comes to the hot drinks offered in a country still closely tied to its British roots, naturally one would expect to find quite a bit in the way of tea. In that expectation I have not been disappointed. However, most people here do take milk in their tea—at least at a dairy farm, they do!

I have to say that as a coffee-drinking American, I was relieved to find my favorite, morning beverage also quite popular here, along with cappuccino, espresso and coffee latte.

Milo, on the other hand, is something totally new to me. We might call it a hot drink similar to cocoa or hot chocolate, but it has more of a malt-like taste.

As for the *Marmite*, now that one raises quite a question mark for American taste-buds. The New Zealanders spread Marmite on their bread or toast the way we might use peanut butter, but take it from me, it doesn't taste *anything* like good ol' *Peter Pan* or *Jiff*!

Marmite is a dark, yeast-based spread with a sharp, salty taste, and it definitely takes some getting used to.

They do have peanut butter here, by the way, as well as *Nutella*—a chocolate-hazelnut spread for which any self-respecting chocoholic would gladly give her eye teeth!

Now when I raise the question of *sultanas*, I'll give you a hint: what they call *Bran and Sultanas* down here, we call *Raisin Bran* back home. You guessed it—a sultana looks just like a raisin to me, but more of a blond one if you want to get technical about it.

And *lollies*? Well, ask any kid what a lolly is, and you might get a different answer every time, but I can guarantee that every one of them will have something to do with candy. I've never known a kid from any culture to turn down a sweet treat, no matter what you want to call it.

You might also be interested to know that the ice cream in New Zealand surpasses any ice cream I've ever eaten anywhere. *Talk about rich!* And flavors I've never heard of before, like Gold Rush, Easter-Egg-Crunch, Jelly-Bean Tip or Hokey Pokey.

Now if you'll excuse me, I have to set the table for "tea" (the meal we ordinarily call supper back in the states). Maybe if I work at it, by the time I get home I'll be able to eat the way they do down here, with a left-handed fork and right-handed knife in the European style of dining.

Oops! I dropped it again.

"Ya' know, it just takes some o' these Yanks a long time to learn how to eat properly, mate!"

123

Dairy Farming in New Zealand

Don your gumboots and get ready to ride! We're off on a motorbike tour of Alan and Jen Topham's 390-acre dairy farm, located near Riverton, New Zealand.

"Hop on," says my Kiwi host, sitting at the ready on his motorcycle with not one, but two dogs perched on behind. This time the yellow lab, Casey, forfeits her seat to me, while herd-dog Jess clings on behind, and we take off for a cross-country ride over the stony ground of this south-island, dairy-farm paradise.

We leave from the overlook of their expansive home, where the Tophams have a phenomenal, panoramic view: mountains stretch from northwest to east in the far distance, with rolling grasslands falling toward a river bottom to the west, and from the south shoreline, nothing but ocean comes between the Topham farm and Antarctica.

Cold, you ask?

Not nearly as cold as you might think, judging from the vegetation in these parts, which leans more toward sub-tropical varieties, believe it or not. Alan and Jen tell me they seldom see a frost here, due to the prevailing weather patterns blowing in from the sea.

That weather *can* roar quite blustery on occasion, is evidenced by last night's gale, which blew out a portion of the Topham hay barn.

On Alan's motorbike, we make a run through numerous grazing paddocks on our way down to take a look at the rocky river bottom, which empties into the ocean. Not only does much of the vegetation we pass look unfamiliar to me, but the bird life I see has no comparison to that back home in Amish country, either.

I *can* recognize a cow when I see one! And as we make our way back up to the open cow shed (we'd call it a milking parlor in the states), the Tophams' dairy herd comes into view—all 350 ladies grazing happily in one of the nearby, 10-acre paddocks.

Dairy farming is handled quite a bit differently here in New Zealand. The entire herd moves daily from one grass paddock to another,

I can recognize a cow when I see one!

eventually rotating over the 40 paddocks on this farm, as the grass growth dictates.

Cows here seldom eat anything but grass, unless drought conditions slow down growth to the degree that the cows need supplemental silage or hay. No grain feeding here.

And when it comes to milking all those bovine beauties, the system Alan and Jen employ definitely puts our dairy operations to shame. They can milk the entire herd of 350 cows in less than two hours' time with a two-sided milking set-up on which they "hook up" 30 cows per side.

Pretty slick, if you ask me, not to mention downright practical. These girls also freshen and dry up all at once, giving the dairy family a much needed break in between. Of course, when calving time comes round, the whole family has to pitch in during that busiest of spring seasons.

Keep in mind that springtime south of the equator comes from September through November, when the Northern Hemisphere normally experiences autumn. Right now, while crocus and daffodil bulbs push their heads up back home, I'm enjoying the crisp apples of fall down here—as well as all the fresh milk I could possibly hope to drink!

Don't get your knickers in a twist!

When you visit another English-speaking country, you'd expect to understand what people have to say, right?

'T'ain't necessarily the case here in New Zealand, where I've had the opportunity to live within a Southland household and experience, first-hand, the innumerable differences in the English language, as spoken by true Kiwis (New Zealanders).

Take simple household terms, for instance. Kiwis do not relax in the living room when they want to stretch out in an easy chair and watch TV; they call that room the *lounge*.

By the way, their television programming not only originates in New Zealand, but quite a few programs come from England (BBC), Australia and the good ol' U.S. of A., as well. Those unavoidable breaks we call commercials, the Kiwis refer to as *adverts* (and I have to tell you, theirs are *much* more interesting).

Now mosey along with me into the kitchen. As you know, we have counter tops in the states, but in New Zealand they call the same thing *benches*. They also use *taps* instead of faucets, and you'll find a switch at every electric plug in the house (for safety reasons, I'm told, since all the power here comes in at 240 volts, rather than the 110 we're accustomed to back home).

So far, I've only gotten myself into trouble when I attempted to cook dinner (a meal which they refer to as *tea*) and I forgot to turn on the master switch that activates the stove. It doesn't do a darn bit of good to turn on a burner, if there's nothing powering the whole stove in the first place!

We've eaten late three times so far—you'd think I'd learn after the first time, now, wouldn't you?

Kitchen utensils here look much the same to me as the ones in my own kitchen, but I did have a little mishap with the potato peeler which caused me to seek the blood-stanching qualities of a **plaster** (that's a Band-Aid® to the uninitiated).

When cooking Kiwi-style, it takes one major change to follow a recipe. You see here, as in most parts of the world, the metric system rules, so ounces and pounds and cups become grams and kilograms and litres.

You also might be interested to know that water does not go down the drain, rather it goes down the plug-hole—which actually does swirl the opposite way in the Southern Hemisphere.

I've also encountered toilets down here that give either a half-flush or a whole flush, depending upon one's need of the moment.

At this juncture, I can't help but insert another unique observation: the *Exeloo*—a completely automated latrine (known as a *loo*), located at strategic points in tourist towns. This thing has an automatic door, an automatic toilet-paper dispenser, automatic flush, sensor-activated hand-washing station (soap, water and blow-dry) and it even automatically locks and self-cleans at preset intervals!

I couldn't stop laughing after I finished up in that one.

Incidentally, tourists over here are affectionately known as *loopies* by the locals. (Pretty accurate description, if you ask me.)

Since we've made it to the traveling stage in this missive, it would seem appropriate to take up the differences in driving, because I still have trouble getting into the wrong side of the cars. In New Zealand the driver sits on the right-hand side of the vehicle, since traffic flows in the opposite direction from that back home.

Let me tell you, it gets the adrenaline pumping to round a corner and see a truck coming at you on what looks to be the wrong side of the road to American eyes!

No, I haven't found the courage to even attempt driving yet. I'm still getting used to looking for road signs on the wrong side of the road. If you threw in shifting gears with the opposite hand and flip-flopping the gas and clutch pedals, I'm absolutely certain I'd end up in the *drain* (that's what they call the ditch over here).

The first time I saw a speed-limit sign I had to do a double-take: it said "100"—not miles per hour, but kilometers per hour.

> *...service attendants still provide service over here—they pump your petrol and carry on a friendly conversation in the process!*

As for the gas stations in New Zealand, they sell *petrol* (not gasoline) by the litre, and at roughly twice the price we pay back home, when you convert the appropriate amount to U.S. gallons. Inflated though our prices may seem to us, they're nothing compared to what Kiwis have to pay to keep their cars on the road.

I have to tell you that service attendants still actually do provide service over here—they pump your petrol for you and carry on a friendly conversation in the process.

Aside from the obvious flip-flop in driving patterns and changes in a few automotive terms (*boot* for trunk, *windscreen* for windshield, and *indicator* for turn signal), once you're actually out on the road, traffic really doesn't seem all that different from the traffic back home.

Locals here chafe at the bit just as much as we do when they're stuck behind a slow-moving *loopie* gawking at the beautiful scenery, so they jump at the chance to *overtake* (pass) whenever they can.

You do not yield to traffic here, either; you must *give way*. And if you don't give way to oncoming traffic, you just might end up in the kind of pickle described by this most interesting traffic sign: *"No Doctor, No Hospital, One Cemetery."*

Take it from me, it's much safer to do a U-turn (perfectly legal here) and get yourself out of harm's way A.S.A.P!

Now if you don't mind, I need to finish my bangers and mash (sausages and mashed potatoes), then go pack my bum-bag so I'm ready for yet another adventure with my Kiwi cohorts.

Tourist adventures abound in Southland

"Yeeeaiiieeeks! We're gonna hit that bridge!"

This screech is barely heard above the double, 350-horse engines powering the jet boat onto which I cling for dear life. But when you're sitting on the outside edge of a boat hurtling itself straight at a bridge abutment at more than 75 kph (kilometers per hour), you don't just sit there with your knuckles turning white.

You YELL!

Welcome to adventure tourism in Queenstown, New Zealand.

On this, my last weekend here in Southland, my Kiwi host treats me to a whirlwind day of adventure tourism in the place which gave birth to that ultimate of adventures—bungee jumping.

Did I do a swan dive off the Kawarau bridge and wait for my eyeballs to pop out, you may ask? Let me just say that if the AJ Hackett Bungee operators would allow a matronly woman with a bad back and a trick knee to attempt such a thing, I definitely would have considered it!

(Lucky for me I had no real choice in the matter.)

Besides, I figured that I'd had entirely enough adventure for one day, after an hour-long, jet boat ride with 360-degree, high-speed turns that barely missed rocks and bridges in the process.

You'd think that when the captain's assistant handed out not only life-jackets, but raincoats before we left the dock, I should have had a clue as to what was coming, right?

It's probably a good thing I came back soaked to the skin in spite of that protective gear, because that way no one could really tell whether my condition originated from the drench of ricocheting water spray or sheer terror (unless they got real close!).

I did enjoy that ride, by the way. But I think they should warn the passenger sitting behind the captain that she needs to duck whenever the captain does. (Toward the end of the ride, I finally got wise and followed suit.)

After recovering from that water-logged experience, we climbed into a mountain-scaling gondola and rode that panoramic contrivance to the very top of Queenstown, where yet another adventure awaited the fool-hardy—I mean, dauntless—tourists: *the Luge*.

Now to anyone who has watched the winter Olympics, you're probably familiar with those bullet-like capsules in which experienced sportsmen hurtle down ice-encrusted tubes at high speeds, to reach the bottom of a mountain without killing themselves in the process.

This particular luge consists of cement runs on which teensy-tiny, open, cart-like sleds roll down a mountainside with wild-eyed tourists clutching onto nothing more than bicycle handles. And they release those tourists on their single-seated vehicles not one at a time at the top, mind you, but *en masse!*

Yes, I did ride this one, but luckily they let crackpots take off all alone at the top, and I had the foresight to stick to the beginner trail all the way to the bottom.

Seriously, while this ride does get exciting, even a small child can handle the foolproof sleds in complete safety. I'd venture to say that the most dangerous part of the whole thing comes when you stand at the ski-style chair-lift down at the bottom, awaiting your next ride to the top.

After surviving a full day of adventure, we topped off my New Zealand experience with a walk in the nearby aviary, where I finally got my first peek at an actual, live Kiwi bird.

In order to see this elusive, flightless bird, you must stay absolutely quiet and wait for your eyes to adjust to the darkness in the night-like habitat building, because these naturally shy, nocturnal birds spook at the slightest of noises.

Our patience and silence paid off, when we witnessed one Kiwi going about his bug-sniffing business, while his partner slept, curled up snuggly by the plate-glass observation window.

Now, after a full, month-long stay at the dairy farm of Alan and Jen Topham, my visit to New Zealand draws to a close. Although I may have had to wait nearly 20 years to make this visit to see my "Kiwi-little-brother" and his family, you can be sure we won't let another 20 go by until we see one another again.

Before I board the plane for my long ride back home, I just have one thing left to figure out: how in blazes do I fit all these souvenirs into one carry-on bag?

Airline travel
or
How long does it take to get your suitcase?

"Sorry, Ma'am, but that flight's been discontinued."

"What?!" says I, twiddling my thumbs after 45 minutes of waiting in line.

"We no longer run that flight to Columbus," says the America West ticketing agent at the check-in desk at the Los Angeles International Airport (LAX). "You'll have to go stand in that other line until we can make arrangements to re-route you through Phoenix. You'll be able to make connections to Columbus from there."

"You gotta be kidding."

Just to let you know, I'd already been on the travel-road for more than 22 hours, and to be honest, I was beginning to get a little punchy—not to mention a teensy bit miffed.

But perhaps I need to start back at the beginning of my trip home from the south end of the south island of New Zealand—a trip that encompassed roughly 9,500 miles and re-crossing the International Date Line.

The whole day had begun off kilter, with the grounding of my very first flight on Ansett Airlines, due to mechanical difficulties. Granted, I'd much rather arrive home *sometime* than not at all, but from that point on, the trip I'd had booked for over two months went downhill fast.

You see, the next available flight from Invercargill to Christchurch didn't leave for three more hours, which presented no real problem for that first leg of my trip.

The problem arose with the second leg, since I had an international connection to make in Auckland (the capitol of New Zealand) on a Quantas flight bound to Los Angeles, CA.

The ticket agent told me that when my second flight landed in Auckland I'd have just 30 minutes to gather up my baggage, transfer from the domestic terminal to the international terminal, check my bags at the Quantas desk, pay my departure tax at the banking window, fill out all the necessary customs forms, then make it through security. (And you *know* what happens when I go through security!)

> *The worst-case scenario: I'd miss my flight and have to stay overnight in Auckland; the best scenario: I'd break a record for the two-mile airport shuffle.*

IF (and that was a *big* if) I managed to accomplish all the aforementioned procedures within the allotted half-hour, *then* I'd have to sprint for the departure gate if I had any hope of boarding that plane before it closed its doors for takeoff.

O.K. So be it.

The worst-case scenario: I'd miss my flight and have to stay overnight in Auckland; the best scenario: I'd break a record for the two-mile airport shuffle.

You'll be happy to know that the first and second legs of my trip to Auckland came off without a hitch. I claimed my luggage from Air New Zealand and re-checked it with Ansett, since I had to change airlines for those first two, re-routed flights. No real difficulty there.

I knew I'd face enough trouble when I landed in Auckland. So I had my running boots on—I was ready!

When the flight landed, I picked up a handy-dandy luggage trolley, then waited at the baggage-claim area for my suitcases. I checked my watch repeatedly while I waited. And I waited. Then I waited some more, until my two, very stuffed-with-treasures bags rolled down the moving beltway.

I grabbed the bags, loaded my trolley, and raced for the front door to hail a cab. The first driver said he couldn't take me—he was parked on the wrong side of the road for pick-ups.

Drats!

I ran across the street in pouring-down rain to find another.

"Is this cab available?"

"Royiiigh-tee-o, Mate."

"Quantas desk, International Terminal—and make it *FAST!*"

"It's not so far, you know, Miss. You can take the shuttle bus from over there."

"You don't understand, my flight's scheduled to leave in 15 minutes, and I can't take time to wait for a bus!"

"Hop in, then." (I could tell he didn't *really* want to get out in the rain to load my suitcases into the trunk. But to his credit, he made a quick job of it. Luckily enough, I had just enough New Zealand dollars left to pay him.)

Well, the good news is that I *did* make my international connection, thanks to a very helpful Quantas agent, who escorted me through the entire, hasty, departure process.

> ...the flight attendant secured the airplane door right behind me!

(I think I must have set a new record for the race to boarding; the flight attendant secured the airplane door right behind me.)

The bad news I must report, however, was that my luggage did *not* make connections with me. When I arrived in Los Angeles twelve-and-a-half hours later, a communiqué awaited saying that my bags would not make it to LAX until the following day.

At least I didn't have to worry about collecting any baggage for the remainder of my journey home...

... which brings us right back to where we started this story:

"The next available flight to Phoenix leaves three hours from now," said the America West attendant. "But that flight's running a half hour late, so when it lands in Phoenix, it looks like you'll have just 10 minutes to make it from the incoming gate to catch your outgoing flight to Columbus."

Should that really surprise me?

I'm relieved to report that I finally made it to Columbus just a little after midnight, more than 30 hours from the time I had begun the long trek back home.

My bags, on the other hand, did not catch up with me until three days later—slightly the worse for wear, I might add, but with their entire contents still intact.

Hallelujah!

Would I make such a trip again?

Youbetcha! But the next time I'll *post* all my souvenirs back home—and you'd better believe I'm gonna make that bungee jump!

Hemisphere flip-flop leaves indelible impressions

Fast-forward from autumn to spring in one day—now there's a jolt to the system!

One would expect to suffer from a bit of jet lag after traversing seven time zones and the International Date Line, but I never gave a thought to season shock.

When I left snow-covered Ohio in early March to travel to the south island of New Zealand, no self-respecting tulip had even begun to think of poking its head above the frosty ground.

But upon my return in early April, I found that I had already missed the crocus and daffodils, not to mention the bloom of a good many tulips to boot.

Funny thing, this hemisphere flip-flop. Until you experience it there's little to prepare a body for its effects.

In addition to the reversed seasons, I also learned that the stars in the Southern Hemisphere really do look quite different from our own, as does the moon—it's upside down, down-under. The constellation Orion (just dipping out of our northern view and peeking into the southern, night skies) looked upside down to me, as well.

The flora and fauna absolutely fascinated me—a good deal of which appeared sub-tropical in nature, even so close to Antarctica. Never before had I seen trees that began their lifecycle with one sort of leaf and developed an entirely different kind of leaf by maturity (e.g Lancewood and several varieties of Gum trees [Eucalyptus]).

Although Kiwis drive on the opposite side of the road, necessitating steering-wheel placement on the opposite side of their vehicles, a tractor is still a tractor no matter what paddock or field you drive it in.

I found that farm folks are pretty much the same no matter how they have to shovel their cow manure, and those who live in a city laugh and cry exactly the same way I do (although I have to admit not always at the same things; I detected a subtle difference in New Zealand humor, which leans more toward that of the British take on life—not nearly so condescending as Americans' humor).

Yet even when you share a common language, differences in accents and slang terms can get you into trouble mighty quick, if you're not careful. But a genuine smile can be understood, no matter what the language.

> *A genuine smile can be understood, no matter what the language.*

It might also interest you to know that Girl Scout cookies are universal (although they're known as *Girl Guide Biscuits* down under) and every good cook knows 101 ways to prepare hamburger (which is mincemeat to a Kiwi) no matter what type of animal it comes from.

Yes, even McDonalds has made it all the way to New Zealand. But we have nothing here that comes close to matching the *Kiwi Burger*—that's a meat patty topped with an egg, sliced beets, fresh cucumber and tomato, along with grated carrots, shredded lettuce and a tasty mayo dressing to top it all off.

Nor does a dessert in any U.S. fast-food-joint come close to matching the *McPav*—a meringue-like puff topped with tangy syrup and chunks of tropical fruits. Quite unique, to say the least.

When it came to food, I thoroughly enjoyed most every dish put before me. But I did have a little trouble eating spaghetti and toast for breakfast. (The baked-beans and toast went down with much less difficulty.)

So, what did I like best about my trip to New Zealand? Without a doubt—the people. Nowhere else have I encountered so many, truly friendly people. From shopkeepers to passers-by on the street, everybody had a kind greeting to offer and appeared eager to help, no matter how curious the request from this crazy Crackpot.

But seeing my "Kiwi little brother" and meeting his family undoubtedly tops my list of "bests." I give special thanks to Alan and Jen Topham, not only for inviting me to come to their south island dairy farm and showing me all the sights from a native's view, but for truly making me feel like a part of the family.

> Grandpa Miller's travel advice: "*take nothing more than a toothbrush, a change of underwear and a pocket-full of money.*"

This *Sadie* (that's a live-in cook/housekeeper/laundry-mistress to the uninitiated) wouldn't have missed her trip for anything the world.

Would I do it all over again?

In a minute! But next time I take my Grandpa Miller's advice to heart: *travel with nothing more than a toothbrush, a change of underwear and a pocket-full of money.*

From A Cockroach To The Captain's Table

Do you remember Captain Stubing of *Love Boat* fame? Well on the Mediterranean Cruise I had the good fortune to take recently, the shiny-domed Captain of our Greek-registered ship, *The Aegean I*, could have passed for Captain Stubing's double.

Though our captain conversed mainly in Greek, he spoke enough English to put his American passengers at ease—and he knew enough elegant flattery to make the jewel-bedecked dowagers swoon.

But entertaining ladies has little to do with running a tight ship. And judging by the efficient crew of *The Aegean I,* and the way she slid expertly into her berth at each port, our Captain certainly knew his starboard from his port.

Now some folks have trouble adjusting to the pitch and yaw of life at sea, but I've never had any real trouble gaining my "sea legs." For an old farm girl it's a cinch—just keep your knees flexed and pretend you're bouncing along trying to keep your balance on a hay wagon. Nothing to it! (You don't have to catch any hay bales, either.)

We were fortunate on this Renaissance Cruise because the weather couldn't have been better nor the seas calmer, for this winter-time of year. Temperatures averaged a high of 65° during the day, and dropped into the mid-50's at night, but sea breezes did make a jacket or sweater most welcome of an evening.

Only one night did our vessel do much rolling to speak of, and that felt quite pleasant after a long day ashore—almost like being rocked to sleep by Neptune, himself. I did notice a few folks who turned a decided shade of green after dinner that evening, but luckily (since I figure I must have been a fish in a previous life) I didn't feel a bit sea sick.

Being anywhere on or near the water has always appealed to me, and, as my best friend Thelma can attest, whenever I get close to anything remotely resembling an ocean habitat, someone needs to keep a close eye on me. At first sign of a dolphin, I'm overboard! (Don't worry, I didn't jump—this time.)

No matter what time of day (or night), you could always find a wonderful spread of food somewhere on board ship, from the early-birds' coffee breakfasts, through formal meal times in the dining room, to afternoon teas and midnight buffets. If you went hungry on this cruise, it certainly was not because you didn't have the opportunity to eat!

I must admit, I did eat my share, but with our rigorous shore excursion schedule, I walked it all off every day. We would dock at a new port each morning, spend the day ashore touring local sights, then get back on board in time for dinner.

Which brings us to "The Captain's Table."

Now considering the number of people on board ship, only a small percentage get lucky enough to rate an invitation to dine with the Captain. You need *connections* of some sort to even be considered. (Owning stock in the cruise line sure couldn't hurt.)

We average, ordinary people watching the "high rollers" up there wining and dining with the big brass have enough trouble just trying to decide which knife and fork go with the salad course and which ones go with the fish course. (The desert fork I had down pat.)

Occasionally Mr. Goodyear did have trouble keeping me from jumping up to serve more coffee to the rest of our dinner companions (old waitressing habits do die hard), although I never could get used to having a waiter actually *stir* my coffee for me.

But one evening I felt right in my own element, when we had a little six-legged visitor scurry across our dinner table. (Remember, you're dealing with a woman who spent two years living in a tipi with all manner of unexpected guests of any species dropping in unannounced.)

In warm climates insects can pose quite a problem, and a ship at sea is no exception to that rule. I can honestly say the other folks at our table didn't share my sympathy toward our visiting cockroach.

Apologizing profusely for the inconvenience, our waiter advised us to report said incident to the cruise line's shipboard representative. And since Mr. Goodyear won the "authoritative-voice contest" hands down, he got to make the presence of our little cucaracha friend known.

Next day, low and behold, what should arrive for us but an invitation to dine at the Captain's Table!

Now some folks would contend that our little bug visitor may have had *something* to do with that summons, but I know the truth: Mr. Goodyear bribed the Captain with a chocolate blimp.

If I'm ever lucky enough to go on another ocean cruise, you can bet your life preserver that I'll stow away a handy-dandy cockroach in my luggage—just to ensure I have an *in* with the captain!

The Dead Sea

Jell-O®.

That's what water in the dead sea feels like—syrupy Jell-O®, after you mix it up and before you put it in the 'fridge to set.

On the recent Mediterranean cruise, that I had the privilege of taking with Mr. Goodyear, we stopped in Israel for a three-day visit. And during our sightseeing time there, we had the opportunity to swim in the Dead Sea.

In case you didn't know (or weren't paying attention in world geography class), the Dead Sea happens to be the lowest point on earth—3,600 feet below sea level. Since it contains nearly 33% salt and minerals, nothing (except a tenacious algae) lives in its environs—hence, the moniker "Dead" sea.

Even though the landscape around that body of water appears mighty desolate and devoid of life, the area is far from dead. Countless hotels and health spas have sprung up along its shores, catering to sun-seeking vacationers, as well as the infirm searching for healing.

You see, since the Dead Sea contains so many minerals, many people claim miraculous recoveries after bathing in its waters—especially those folks plagued by tormenting skin conditions.

That demand for skin-itching relief has also given birth to another lively industry—health and beauty products made from those very salts and minerals.

And don't forget the sea's "black mud," which is reputed to make one's skin smooth as a newborn baby's. Naturally, I *had* to bring some home to try. (I'll let you know how it works.)

Of course, after traveling thousands of miles to visit the Dead Sea, we couldn't leave without taking a little dip in its famous waters—even if the mercury had only hit 69 degrees in the sunshine! Needless to say, we cut the outdoor portion of our swim mighty short and quickly headed inside the hotel to warm up in the hot tub!

By the way, in case you're wondering—all the hype about the Dead Sea is true; anyone can float in those mineral-rich waters. Like a proverbial cork. But take it from me, you DON'T want to get your face wet. It makes the eyes sting like crazy, and it doesn't taste too

> *...anyone can float in those mineral-rich waters, like a proverbial cork.*

great, either, not a bit like sea-water; it's much saltier, yet bitter at the same time. (I just HAD to taste it, doncha know!)

My skin felt so smooth after that little swim, I can understand why so many people with skin conditions like to bathe in those waters. It took three showers before I could finally work up a good lather with a bar of soap!

On the way back to the ship, our guide also pointed out the Qumran Caves, located in the desert near Dead Sea. In some of those caves the famous Dead Sea Scrolls lay hidden in pottery jars for nearly two-thousand years, before a Bedouin shepherd boy discovered them while hunting for lost sheep.

Those scrolls, the oldest known biblical manuscripts in the world, are kept in a special museum in Jerusalem, where scholars still study their contents. (No, we didn't have time to go see the scrolls—this time.)

If you could see the landscape in the vicinity of those caves and realize how many more caves must stretch for miles and miles in all directions, I'm sure that you, too, would wonder just what other treasures might lay hidden in those dark caverns.

Anyone up for some spelunking? Or how about an archaeological dig? I always have had a fascination for digging in the dirt in search of ancient artifacts.

We certainly saw a broad range of archaeological digs in progress in every country we visited throughout the Mediterranean's cradle of civilization.

Next, I'll tell you about—Masada, mountain-top fortress built by Herod the Great, where 967 Jewish Zealots held off more than 10,000 Roman soldiers for over a year during the Roman occupation of Judea. Just wait till you hear what happened there!

Masada

Perched high upon a mountain top, overlooking the parched lands along the Dead Sea in Israel, stand the remains of a 2000-year-old desert fortress called Masada.

Of all the historic places I've had the good fortune to visit during my recent trip to the cradle of civilization, taking the cable-car up the mountain and walking around the dusty ruins of Masada has moved me the most.

For upon that mountain, 967 Jewish Zealots held off more than 10,000 Roman soldiers for over a year, during the Romans' complete occupation of Judea in the first century A.D., after they'd finally destroyed the Jewish Temple in Jerusalem.

Those odds seem to appear a bit lop-sided, no? But wait until you hear "the rest of the story." (My apologies to Paul Harvey, for I mean no trespass upon his territory.)

First, we need a little background information about Masada before you can appreciate the whole saga:

King Herod the Great (infamous in Biblical history for causing the slaughter of all Jewish infants under the age of two in Bethlehem) had the mountain top fortress built as a last stronghold in case someone tried to overthrow his kingdom.

To say he was a bit paranoid is an understatement, since he had most of his potential adversaries killed—including his wife and children—not to mention all those babies, any one of whom could have been the *King of the Jews*.

But despite Herod's madness, he did have a gift for construction, and what the archaeologists uncovered at Masada proved it.

I'd guess the top of that mountain covers roughly five or six acres, and he turned that dusty, waterless promontory into a completely-walled, self-contained complex that could sustain a population of 1000 people for up to 50 years—without anyone having to come down off that mountain.

Herod built a complete town up there (including palaces and synagogue, bathhouses and swimming pools), and he designed the place to withstand any siege he could conceive.

An army coming against him would have no water source in the desert below; they would have only what water they could carry. With the system Herod installed atop Masada, defenders could taunt a besieging army below (when its water began to run low), by throwing that precious wet stuff over the mountain sides.

That could be enough to dishearten any thirsty soldier.

Herod's water cisterns alone are a work of unparalleled genius. He had not one or two, but 14 cisterns (each one bigger than my house!) carved out of the sheer rock of the mountain. Together with a system of trenches and ditches, Herod could catch precious run-off in his cisterns from as far away as Jerusalem during the rainy season.

In addition, he also had huge storehouses built that contained enough food to sustain his people for 50 years. Archaeologists uncovered pottery jars the size of a small child, that bore inscriptions of their contents and the countries of their origin—for example, dried fruit came from Egypt and fine wines from Cypress and Spain.

Now picture those well-provisioned Jewish Zealots, perched high on their mountain-top fortress, pitted against those 10,000 well-armed (although thirsty) Roman soldiers, determined to crush the rebels' resistance.

The year, 72 A.D.; the setting, in the Yehuda desert along the west bank of the Dead Sea.

The Zealots, whose numbers included women and children, controlled all three winding paths leading up the sheer, rock face of that mountain. However the wily Roman General decided to build a siege ramp up the side of that mountain in order to drive his battering rams and war machines right up to the Zealots' front door and bash it down.

"But couldn't those Zealots kill the Roman workers as they piled rocks and stones higher and higher," may you ask?

145

Good question.

Guess who the General used to build the ramp? Jewish slaves. He knew that the rebels on top of Masada would not dare kill their own people.

In fact, whenever the Zealots tried to interrupt or thwart the progress of that ramp (or when they decided to taunt the thirsty Romans below by splashing water down the mountain side), General Silva would choose ten or twenty Jewish slaves and have his men cut off their heads. Then he'd load those heads onto his catapults and shoot them right up into the heart of Masada.

That put a quick end to interference with the siege ramp.

> *It took the Roman general over a year to complete his ramp... the Jewish rebels, could do nothing more than watch and wait.*

It took the Roman general just over a year to complete his ramp. And during all that time, the Jewish rebels, under the leadership of El'azar, could do nothing but watch and wait.

When General Silva breached the first wall, El'azar knew the following day would mark the end of Masada. The tenacious Jews had no escape. They were outnumbered ten to one.

But the next morning, when Silva's Romans broke through fortress' gate, they had a disappointing letdown.

They found the Jewish Zealots already dead; all their possessions burned and destroyed. For rather than let the Romans loot and plunder and carry off their women and children as slaves, the Zealots chose to take their own lives and die as free men.

Here's a portion of El'azar's last words to his people:

"My loyal followers, long ago we resolved to serve neither the Romans nor anyone else, but only God... It is evident that daybreak will end our resistance, but we are free to choose an honorable death with our loved ones. Let our wives die unabused, our children without knowledge of slavery; after that, let us do each other an ungrudging kindness, preserving our freedom... It will be a bitter blow to the Romans, that I know, to find our persons beyond their

reach and nothing left for them to loot. One thing only let us spare—our store of food; it will bear witness when we are dead to the fact that we perished not through want, but because, as we resolved at the beginning, we chose death rather than slavery... Come! While our hands are yet free and can hold a sword, let them do a noble service. Let us die unenslaved by our enemies and leave this world as free men in company with our wives and children."

(As recorded by Roman historian Josephus)

The men drew lots to choose ten among themselves who would kill all the rest; then those ten drew lots to choose the last one to kill the other nine before falling upon his own sword to complete the grizzly task.

How do we know this, if the Romans found all the Zealots dead?

They also found a woman and several children alive, who'd hidden themselves in one of the mountain's cisterns, and historian Josephus recorded their horrifying tale.

Archaeologists also found the potshards those Zealots had used to choose their killers. And the rest of their finds on that mountain top fortress confirmed the whole story of Masada.

The spot holds a powerful place in the unfolding annals of Jewish history.

Next—*Jerusalem:* a city held sacred by three major religions of the world, and one they continue to fight over to this day.

Jerusalem: The Holy City

"Five dollars! Five dollars! Nice book. Pretty pictures. Lovely souvenir. You take home, yes?"

"No thanks. I don't have room to pack one more book."

"Post cards. Have plenty postcards. Ten for dollar. See? Nice pictures. How 'bout necklace. Pretty necklace, one dollar."

Each time the tour bus came to a stop on my recent visit to Israel, native hawkers stood at the ready with all manner of postcards and trinkets, wood carvings or camel rides—all meant to part tourists from their precious American dollars.

We found it no different in Jerusalem. If anything, the souvenir vendors there seemed to stick even tighter. They stuck so tight, in fact, that our guides warned us repeatedly to keep a firm grip on our purses and wallets, as we took in the historic sights of the *Holy City.*

That was quite a challenge, however, when walking through crowded streets of old Jerusalem. And yes, the old city really does look much the way it must have looked during biblical times— narrow, winding streets; merchants and vendors set up in every nook and cranny; donkeys, children (and small cars) vying for space on the crowded walkways.

If you closed your eyes, you could almost imagine yourself on the same street 2,000 years before, donkey brays and all.

But even though Herod's ancient walls still surround the heart of old Jerusalem, the new city bears little resemblance to its predecessor.

High-rise buildings cover all the hills surrounding the old city, and the hustle and bustle of modern commerce clogs the streets with rush-hour traffic jams.

Oh, we got to see our fill of the so-called "holy sights" while there. But I doubt if Jesus would recognize any of them, were He to walk or sit or pray in those same spots today.

At least one church (if not three or four) covers every piece of land revered as holy by the Christians: for example, the Church of the Holy Sepulcher on Golgotha, Church of all Nations at Gethsemane, etc., etc.

> *I doubt if Jesus would recognize any of them, were He to walk or sit or pray in those same spots today.*

In Bethlehem (now a suburb of Jerusalem) the Church of the Nativity covers a grotto (underground cave) that most people accept as the birthplace of Christ.

But to get down to that grotto, one must walk through two smoky churches (one seemingly inside the other), both dark, dank and filled with the stench of incense and lamp-oil, before you even come to the steps that lead to the cave.

And when you finally get down there, the whole thing's so full of altars and candles and oil lamps and gold and silver icons (pictures), that it's hard to recognize it as a cave, let alone find a place to stand when a bus load of tourists descends en-mass.

If you're the least bit claustrophobic, or have any difficulty breathing in a smoky atmosphere, it's definitely NOT a place to go on purpose.

A silver star with a hole in it marks the spot where Mary supposedly gave birth. If you crawl down there and look through that hole, you can glimpse a piece of rock from the original cave.

Frankly, knowing the exact spots Christ was born or died or prayed means little to me; knowing that He WAS born means everything.

One of the things I did find most interesting in Jerusalem is a place held most dear in Jewish tradition—the *Western Wall*—better known as the *Wailing Wall* to Gentiles.

Orthodox Jews still come to stand and pray at that holiest of spots, which is all that remains of the old temple built by King Solomon to house the Ark of the Covenant.

The Western Wall stood as the back wall in the *Holy of Holies,* hence the closest tangible link left to that holiest of spots for the Jews. Some even claim that if you touch it, you can feel a tingling sensation emanating from the wall.

I touched it, but I didn't feel a thing. I did feel something when I squeaked a finger through the fence to touch a 2,000-year-old olive tree in the Garden of Gethsemane, though. I really wanted to climb that tree and sit up there for a while; a high fence protects those trees from crazy tourists like me.

All in all, the Jerusalem experience was quite enlightening. And when I climbed back aboard that bus, exhausted at the end of our day, a few wily vendors had more American dollars than they had started out with that day.

"One dollar! One dollar! Big picture Jerusalem. You take home. Yes?"

"No more pictures."

"Two pictures, one dollar. Last Chance!"

Would anyone be interested in a nice, panoramic color photo of the city of Jerusalem? I do have an extra one to spare.

Gentle Creatures Of The Sea

Three bottlenose dolphins, Thunder, Sheri and her baby Echo, accompanied me in the most wonderful swim of my life recently, at *Theater of the Sea* located in Islamorada on the Florida Keys.

Swimming with the dolphins has fulfilled one of my lifelong dreams, and—as dreams often have a wont to do—it flew by entirely too fast.

At *Theater of the Sea,* the Dolphin swim programs are booked months in advance. Each swim time lasts one-half hour, with 45 minutes of instruction before one can enter the water with these 300 to 500-lb. animals. Six of us had to share one swim time, as well, so the whole half-hour did not belong to me, alone.

We were all careful to follow the trainer's instructions, making sure not to swim in one portion of the dolphins' habitat. If they chose not to participate in the "people swim," they could swim away into their own space.

But being naturally curious creatures, they spent the entire swim time thoroughly checking us all out.

What an incredible experience!

They glided by so effort-lessly and literally swam rings around us humans. We had the chance to "get a ride" by holding on to the dorsal fins of two dolphins, and we were allowed to touch their sides, being careful not to touch heads, bellies or tail flukes.

> *...a dolphin feels slippery and springy—like a giant, hard-boiled egg.*

Ever wonder what a dolphin feels like? Slippery and springy—like a giant, hard-boiled egg.

In case you didn't know, you can tell individual dolphins apart by their dorsal fins; each one being different from another. Sheri's was fairly smooth, and Thunder's had a small notch in the back.

Baby Echo's, smaller and completely smooth. I called them each by name every time they swam by me.

I couldn't get over the incredible gentleness of these giant mammals. They could kill a man with one ramming blow if they wanted to. Yet, even in captivity, they're so forgiving—and so intelligent; they often seem to be the ones training their people!

If I wrote about dolphins for the next several months, I still couldn't tell you all there is to know about these ocean-going cetaceans.

After swimming next to these three dolphins and looking them in the eyes, I'm convinced they're much more civilized creatures than we human beings claim to be.

Theater of the Sea, P.O. Box 407, Islamorada, FL 33036, 305-664-2431.

On the road again!

(Think Willie Nelson here…)
"On the road again. I just can't wait to get on the road again…

"Have camper, will travel," is my motto, "Gypsy Grandma" is my name!

Well, when your grandbabies live all over the place, what other choice does a love-starved "Brraamma" have?

Luckily, thanks to that good ol' bag of miracles, I just happen to have a little Toyota mini-motorhome at my disposal and a handy travel buddy in the form of my ding-bat Chocolate Lab-Dalmatian, Roxie.

She may not have all her marbles, but she definitely makes a great companion for a woman traveling alone.

I ask you, who's gonna bother a middle-aged matron when she's trying to control a 70+-pound pooch on springs? No one who has an ounce of self-preservation in his make-up, that's for darn sure!

And I can tell you something else, when it comes to spending nights alone on the road, I have no qualms whatsoever with Roxie along. NOTHING happens in the vicinity of my little camper that I don't know about *instantly.* Roxie may not have much in the way of common sense, but she does have perfect canine-radar for danger—and to Roxie, EVERYTHING means danger.

She's the biggest chicken dog ever born.

That attribute can serve a woman on the road quite handily. *I* don't have to worry about fearing anything, cuz she does it all for me! Besides, giving in to fright or panic is a big waste of energy, as far as I'm concerned. It also deprives one of meeting some mighty interesting people along the way.

I've learned that when you expect the best out of people, that's usually what you're apt to encounter, but when you do nothing but fear the worst, you likely will find exactly what you fear.

> I've learned that when you expect the best out of people, that's usually what you're apt to encounter; when you fear the worst, you likely will find exactly what you fear.

So why waste precious time dealing with all that negative energy when you can be having a wonderful time instead?

For as we all know, the road definitely means adventure, and I'm ready to embark upon another one!

But first, I have to check the air pressure in my tires, make sure all the fluid levels in the engine are topped off, fill the freshwater tank, get the little 'fridge cranked up and filled, and load all the "stuff" I have to take to the grandbabies.

How can any self-respecting grandma arrive without a few presents, I ask?

I also need to fill the dog-food container, ready the traveling kennel, situate the fan so Roxie doesn't expire in the heat, and secure the tie-down cable so I don't have a dog jumping into my lap at the first sudden stop.

Hey, I think I've got this travel stuff down pat. Give me a few snacks and a water jug within handy reach, and I'm READY!

"On the road again... Just can't wait to get on the road again."

A Penguin's Odyssey,
or
Vernon comes home for Christmas

You've heard the old, old story—about humanity and glory,
How the glamour and the glitz of life blind those who will not see.
Now I heard another version—'bout a Penguin they call Vernon.
So I'll spin his Odyssey for you, to warm your hearts this 'eve.

Our story begins on the front step of Lee's Penguin Grill in downtown Loudonville, way back in 1993, where Vernon held the job of "door-penguin." His duties were fairly simple and straightforward, really—greet the customers and make them feel at home. No pretense, no glib remarks. Simple tasks for an unflappable, gregarious penguin like Vernon.

But Vernon had a problem.

Oh, he liked his job well enough. But sitting there on that front step day after day, as Vernon watched all manner of people come and go, he wondered where, exactly, *did* they go? Vernon yearned to follow them and explore beyond the world of Lee's front stoop.

In the manner of all true seekers, one night in the fall of that fateful year, Vernon deserted his post and disappeared from Loudonville, to hit the road on a quest for high adventure.

The penguin friends he left behind just couldn't understand his sudden departure, for as grouping birds (flightless though they be) they could not fathom how one penguin all alone could survive out in the scary world for very long.

When two years passed with no news from Vernon, they held a penguin wake to his memory—giving one whale of a party in his honor; the town still talks about it.

But Vernon's friends underestimated his pluck and resourcefulness; they gave up on him much too quickly, as this story (in Vernon's own words) of his adventuresome quest will attest.

In case you're wondering how I came to know the details of this tale—I must tell you I got it straight from the penguin's beak when he turned up on my door step last week, asking for a glass of ice-water.

"I aimed to travel the world in search of the place where I belonged," said Vernon, chomping on a piece of ice. "It all started out in the fall of '93 when I hopped aboard a hot-air balloon and decided to take it wherever the winds would blow (mostly south at that time of year).

"After hitting a high wire and crash-landing in the Mississippi River near St. Louis, I floated with the current for a few days and ended up in New Orleans. (They pronounce it 'N'orrrrrlins' down there.) I hooked up with a character by the name of Charley, a mule who pulled a tourist surrey around the 'old town'. He had me sit up next to the driver and give folks the inside scoop on Basin Street and Jackson Square. It turned out to be a great winter job.

"In the spring, I signed on as an ice-polisher for the crew of the *Enchanted Seas*—a cruise ship that traveled all over the Caribbean, stopping in Jamaica, Cozumel, and other tropical-type islands in the area.

"While on shore leave in the Cayman Islands, I met up with an old friend, Theodore Tortoise, whom I'd known when I was a young chick in southern waters off the coast of South America. He told me he thought I had better go find my parents, since they didn't look too great the last time he'd seen them.

"So I jumped ship and headed south, stopping off at a few tourist-ruins along the way. (The tourists were not in ruins, rather they *visited* the ruins—ancient Mayan, most of them.)

"But I reached home too late. Father and Mother had departed for the next world before I got a chance to tell them goodbye. Despondent, I hit the high seas once more, swimming anywhere the tides would take me.

"One day I ran into a of couple bottle-nosed dolphin acquaintances who warned me of renegade pirates in the area," Vernon continued, "but in my grief, I ignored their warnings.

"The next day while scouting for a little breakfast in a nearby school of sunfish, got tangled up in a net and found myself hauled to the surface, facing the ugliest pirate I'd ever seen—*Gray Bart*.

"He gave me a choice: turn pirate or become whale fodder. Needless to say, I chose a life of piracy. For the next two years we sailed the globe, and in the process I got to visit distant relatives from New Zealand to the Antarctic shores.

"When we reached the Mediterranean Sea in early '95, Greek fishermen rammed our ship, boarded, and forced our crew to choose between eating 10 lbs. of baklava or walking the plank. Being a reasonably proficient swimmer, I jumped and ended up washing ashore along the coast of Turkey three weeks later.

"Since I was in the neighborhood, I decided to make a pilgrimage to Jerusalem, so I hitched a ride on a nearby camel and spent the next month learning to enjoy the taste of sand.

"I never did get used to all those small children following the tourists everywhere trying to hawk olive-wood mangers at every bus and camel stop. But I did rather enjoy dancing the Macarena with our Turkish Camel Driver!

"After seeing all the sites around Jerusalem, then working for a time mining Dead Sea chemicals (that water made my feathers very smooth), I finally found a job in shipping and signed on as a fruit inspector on a freighter heading west for the Atlantic and the good ol' U.S. of A.

"When we hit the Florida coast, I left the ship, hitched a ride on the Goodyear Blimp, and figured that I'd land back in Ohio somewhere in the vicinity of Akron. But would you believe it? I found myself in San Antonio, Texas, instead!

"It was there that I got mixed up with a couple of sidewalk circus-types who talked me into joining their juggling act as they headed further west. They juggled me, a bowling ball and three apples, taking a bite from each apple as it came around. I only got bit once; they never did that again.

"We made our way as far as a Native American reservation in the Oklahoma panhandle, where we became honorary members of the Witchawaychigo tribe. (They told me I reminded them of a feathered armadillo.)

"Wandering further west we soon found ourselves in Las Vegas with no more in our pockets than two TicTacs, a Clark bar, and $2.87 in small change. Since most of the activity on the Las Vegas strip happens away from the sidewalks, I left the juggling troupe and took a job waiting tables in one of the swanky restaurants at *The Mirage*. (I spent break times down by the dolphin habitat; made me feel more connected to my roots, doncha know.)

"That's where I ran into Wally—my long-lost pelican buddy. He had a job hot-wiring slot machines for little old ladies in out-of-the way casinos. (You have to watch out for those ladies... er... women when you approach machines they happen to claim as their own. I ran into one with a mighty wicked left hook.)

"Wally and I decided to throw our resources into one basket, so to speak, and after we got a few bucks ahead, we blew Vegas and headed for Tahoe, where the water was clear and money flowed faster than the Mohican River at flood stage.

"But in the fall of '96, Wally succumbed to gambling fever, went bust (even going so far as to lose his glass eyeball to pay gambling debts) and ended up convalescing in a gambler's anonymous halfway-house in Reno.

"That New Year's Eve—all alone in the crowd—I made up my mind to head to the West Coast."

"On the first day of '97, I hitch-hiked with a friendly trucker as far as Hollywood, and I went to work in a mall, polishing floors after hours. (Always did love all that sliding!)

"When I finally earned enough money for bus fare, I bought a ticket to the San Francisco Bay area and went to work for a tie-die T-shirt shop in Berkeley. (You wouldn't believe what you see on the streets of Berkley these days!)

"On weekends, I took the BART to *Fisherman's Wharf* in San Francisco, where I set up a barbecue on a houseboat in the marina and sold grilled shrimp by the pound to earn a little extra spending money.

"But 'long about spring, I began to feel the itch to go back to Loudonville. For no matter how many people I met, nor how many places I traveled, nowhere did I feel the kind of acceptance and love that I'd felt among my penguin pals back at Lee's Grill.

"So later that summer, when I finally had enough to afford a plane ticket, I took a flight out from the San Francisco airport heading east. I was on my way back home to Ohio—or so I thought.

"Unfortunately, a tornado caught us somewhere over the vicinity of Kansas, and after a considerable amount of huffing and puffing, it deposited us high in the mountains of Montana. The survivors rappelled our way down the mountain, and when we reached civilization, I swore that no one would ever—repeat—they'd NEVER get me off the ground again!

"In Montana I had enough money left to buy a bus ticket, so I headed east on a nice, boring Greyhound, eating my meals from junk food machines in various bus terminals along the route until we hit Chicago.

"I ran out of money in Chicago and needed some quick cash, so I signed on as a kiddy ride on the merry-go-round near *Wrigley Field*. (A little known fact: kids always pick penguin seats when all the horses are taken.)

"While in Chicago, I wandered down to the stock yards on weekends to pick up pig snouts. (Did you know that barbecued, they're quite a delicacy there? Set me up a barbe' once again and made a little more money after ball games.)

"When I finally had earned enough to rent a car and buy gas, I started the drive back to Loudonville, where I hoped my old friends at Lee's Penguin Grill had not forgotten me.

"For you see, when I frequented the neighborhood of the Chicago stock yards, I ran into Wilbert the pig, who in his great wisdom said, *'If you ain't figured it out yet, Bug-eyes, you should know that nobody'll ever treat you better than the old gang back home'.*"

And that's how I came to hear Vernon's story—after he hit a buck-deer just west of the Mohican Forest, totaled his rental car and came waddling up my driveway asking for a drink of water and a Hershey bar.

Now you may think this story sounds a trifle bit fabricated, but I'll have you know that Vernon pulled pictorial proof from among the souvenir-type mementos he carried in his backpack.

And you can see that proof for yourself if you visit The Penguin Grill in downtown Loudonville. Tell Lee you've come to see Vernon the Penguin, who came home for Christmas. He'll be glad to make you feel right at home—Vernon that is.

He got his old job back, I'm told. And the whole gang threw him a big party—even bigger than the one they threw for his wake.

It's quite an accomplishment to come back from the dead; though the gang *had* given him up their minds—they'd never *completely* let him go in their hearts.

ABOUT THE AUTHOR:

MaryLee Marilee
(With a name like that, how can I help but spread a little sunshine!)

Think of *The Crackpot* (MaryLee Marilee) as a cheerleader for the human spirit—a light shining through the cracks of her resurrected pot that helps to keep folks moving forward, instead of wandering alone in the dark. *"Heaven knows, even the best of us need a little encouragement to keep on keepin' on."*

After moving 19 times, raising three kids, and living in too many homes to count (including a tipi), ML now lives full time in her 26' motorhome, traveling coast to coast visiting her grand-children.

Call her a glorified "bag lady" if you will!

"In my own hair-brained way, I do my best to help folks
find a smile while coping with the foul-balls
life has a way of zinging at us."

Contact ML at   **Maryleemarilee@gmail.com**   or
Marylee@Hearthstones.net

www.ingramcontent.com/pod-product-compliance
Lightning Source LLC
Chambersburg PA
CBHW061721020426
42331CB00006B/1038